The Ultimate

L⊙CAL
MARKETING
SYSTEM

**The 10-Step System For Generating A Bucket Load
Of Leads Into Your Business... Every Month**

Books may be purchased by contacting the publisher and author at:

Go Websites
Parkside House
12A Swan Street
Sileby
Leicestershire
LE12 7NW

Publisher: Go Websites
First Edition

DISCLAIMER

The contents of this book do not constitute individual advice to the reader. The ideas, procedures and suggestions contained in the book are not intended as a substitute for consulting with a professional business advisor. Neither the authors nor publisher shall be held liable or responsible for any loss or damage allegedly arising from any information or suggestion in this book.

CONTENTS

CHAPTER 1

Introduction

As the owner of a small business, what would you say is the one thing stopping you from getting to that next level? There might be a number of short-term obstacles like not having enough hours in the day, staff issues, a backlog of work, cash flow problem; but what is stopping you from fixing those issues, and genuinely making progress?

The more business owners I talk to, the more frequently I hear the same root barrier. It always comes back to the generation of sales leads, more people getting in touch looking to do business with you, and more existing customers returning again and again. What's more, it's often not a massive burst of customers that is desired, but a steady and consistent supply of quality leads flowing into your business each month.

Having a predictable supply of leads means you can be more selective with the projects you choose to accept, be more confident to raise your prices, hire extra members of staff and ultimately free up more of your time to work on the things you enjoy most.

Now I'm guessing by the fact that you are reading this book, you're still on the search for a way to generate a bigger supply of new business opportunities.

If this is the case, then I'm guessing that everything you've tried in the past hasn't generated the kind of results which either the person or company selling it to you had initially promised, or which you'd secretly hoped. Whether it's your previous web designer, a local newspaper, Google, or even perhaps courses you've been on and books you've read, nothing you've tried seems to work that well.

Don't beat yourself. You are no different to the majority of business owners in the world. We're a unique breed of people who are not afraid of hard work, putting in long hours or going without life's pleasures like holidays and weekends, in the name of investing in the business and a better future.

Now there are many places you can learn about aspects of running a business, but it turns out no one will teach you the exact techniques needed to build a website that actually works at driving in leads. You just muddle on by, looking at what everyone else does and most likely trying things that never seem to work.

If your plan is to keep doing the same things you've always done, or worse yet, keep doing nothing but hoping for a magically different outcome, then you may well be disappointed. Have you ever said to yourself, "we will increase the amount of advertising we do when we're in a better financial position", or "we'll get that campaign launched when we have a bit more time?"

I have some bad news. Unless you're actively working on improving those things NOW, that day will likely never arrive. You'll never have enough time to focus on growing your business, or you'll never have the excess budget you're hoping for.

Before you know it, the years have flown by and it starts to feel that even though you've been running and running month after month, you've really only been on a treadmill and never actually covered any ground.

Alternatively, perhaps you have invested? You've invested good pound after bad into advertising and marketing that just hasn't worked, and you're just not prepared to keep pouring your hard-earned profits down the drain any more.

Most small businesses who have their sights on climbing a mountain, never actually get out of the woods and ascend to any height at all. They sadly never even get to stop, look back over their shoulder and enjoy the breath-taking views.

Before we get started, I'd like you to take a moment to think about what success means to you. What is your mountain? Why are you attempting to climb? It's your vision for success which becomes the most substantial reason for getting your business heading in the right direction.

Your definition of success will be different from mine, which will be different from the next person's. Is it merely to provide a decent monthly income so that you can take care of your family and afford regular holidays, or do you intend to scale your brand and become a national or international market leader?

Some people are drawn towards the money, fancy cars, big houses, whilst others are in search of freedom, with time to focus on experiences during early retirement. There's no right or wrong answer to this and whatever goal you choose is completely fine.

I'm sure you don't want to be that person who spends all of their hours working on the business, with nothing to show for it at the end of their journey. Or worse yet, regretting all of the priceless hours that they never spent playing with their children or enjoying the company of family and friends.

Most small businesses which fail, do so not because their product or service wasn't good enough, not because an external problem affected their industry, not even because of cash flow problems (like they would tell you). It's because they woke up one morning and decided "enough is enough". That little flame that burns deep in their belly faded and went out. They just weren't prepared to keep struggling without getting the rewards they deserved for their hard work and determination over the years.

Now, I'm not suggesting for a minute that your small business is struggling (again, each of our definitions of struggling will be different too), but statistically speaking the majority of small business owners are not satisfied with their current situation.

The good news is that in this book, I'm going to share with you our experience of working with hundreds of small businesses and for the first time ever, reveal our 10-step system for ensuring that any small business can succeed to generate a consistent flow of new and returning customers.

The best thing is, this system has been created from deep within the trenches, not based on theory or idealism. We've tried and failed more times than we dare remember, but with each one of those scars we've moved nearer to having a system based solely on the principle of 'what works'. We have proven this across many different industries, from hotels to builders, plumbers to estate agents, financial services to taxi companies, sports equipment installers to mechanics, wedding caterers to scrap yards, and the list goes on.

What's more, these are the exactly the same marketing systems that we have used to grow our own business. Having started out as Splendid Apple, a micro-business in a stuffy backroom office with just Lee and I, to a thriving marketing organisation and winner of the 2018 SBS Award by BBC Dragon's Den Star, Theo Paphitis.

More and more of your competitors are seeing the value in digital marketing, and recognising it as the future for lead generation and sales. They are beginning to invest more money and time than ever before and not only getting this working but are beginning to pull away from the rest of the pack and more importantly from you.

If you have a system which consistently generates a steady flow of leads, imagine how this will impact your business and your life. Not having to take on problem projects, no discounting in order to win work. Not having to think of energy draining marketing campaigns to hit your sales targets or every time the pot is running low. You could perhaps justify hiring new staff or contractors to get the work done and get some established systems in place so that work can be done to the same standard each and every time. You will finally have time to spend working on the business or time to take those holidays that are long overdue.

What's more, you can finally start to feel and act like the business owner you truly are. You can stand up proudly to your family, friends and peers as they see a successful business owner who is achieving great things in their life, not a busy fool who is investing the best years of his or her life by flogging what starts to look to others like a dead horse!

You'll be able to have a business that provides for your life, not a life that provides for your business. Feel the freedom to enjoy your work and work on the things you choose to. Take the business in the direction you feel best, not being reactive to short-term problems which not having enough cash or leads might bring. Being able to take some mental space from your business and be truly present as your children and family grow up, not having to work late or always be thinking about work and forever feeling guilty.

How will this book help my business?

It's a smart question, and believe me, we understand more than most people that your time is incredibly precious, so I want to start by outlining this from the word go.

As business owners, Lee and I believe that actions speak louder than words. This book is designed to be short, concise and inspirational to the small business owner who knows there has to be a better way but is just yet to find it.

For many, this book will be like switching a light on in an otherwise completely dark room, to light up and reveal a clear path to success.

In this book you will discover:

- Each of the 10 stages of the local marketing system for generating more leads
- Real-life actionable steps for success
- A detailed explanation of how you or your web designer can implement these strategies
- Complete understanding of why this stuff works to improve your marketing knowledge

Make notes in the book and revisit the book regularly as a reference guide, but above all, be sure to take action fast and often. If there are any certainties in business, it's that things will take more time than you imagined and will be harder than you might have expected.

I'd recommend that you approach this book in a positive way and to remain open-minded throughout. Try to avoid thinking "Oh, I've seen things like this before" or "this won't work for my business", because like I've already described, we've had success with this in all types of businesses of all shapes and sizes. It's not a quick-win tactic, but a more long-term formula for predictable results.

CHAPTER 2

Success Story

Back in 2011, and not long after Lee and I had started Splendid Apple, we began working with a customer in Leicester who operated an apartment lettings business. The Managing Director, had been recommended to us by one of our existing customers (incidentally our first customer ever).

When we first met, the business was struggling from the after-effects of the recession and the 'property slump', with an incredibly worrying 25% of their 224 apartments currently lying unoccupied. The financial implications of having 56 empty apartments at an average of £580 in monthly rent, means a total of £389,760 in lost annual revenue every single year!

They felt like they were banging their heads against the wall. After all, they were already spending handsome sums of money doing everything they could to get those empty rooms occupied. Their current mix of advertising included full-page adverts in the Yellow Pages, further adverts in local newspapers, working with local and online lettings agents and a small brochure website.

The website was a pretty typical website you might have expected to see from a property management company at the time. There was a slideshow effect which rotated through some nice images of the swimming pool, sauna and gym, together with a precise description of the facilities you could expect to receive as a tenant. There was also a 'contact us' page where people could get in touch with their enquiries.

Now the business undoubtedly had an excellent product. The apartments were varying sizes, with modern decor, fully furnished rooms, an incredible City Centre location right at the heart of the City's Cultural Quarter. Even with all the facilities and features, they still had 56 empty rooms, and could only put this down to the market and the 'economy'.

Having initially beed quite sceptical as to how online marketing would help, the Managing Director felt he'd literally tried everything, so there was nothing more he had to lose. Having had his fingers burnt with other advertisers in the past, he was naturally cautious.

Preferring to wait for some initial results rather than going all out for a new website, we started out just working on an SEO (search engine optimisation) campaign aiming to move their website higher up in the Google rankings for terms which would likely attract new prospects and leads.

After only a few months the progress was already evident, and the number of new leads via the website had risen from a handful a month to around 23. Still not satisfied with this, we soon got to work on building a new website in a style which we predicted would lend itself to attracting even more leads.

Through the deployment of what turned out to be an early version (although we didn't know it at the time) of our local marketing system, within the first year we were able to not only increase monthly enquiries from an average of 23 per month to 119 (That's an impressive 417% increase) we were also able to fill almost all of the apartments on an ongoing basis due to having a predictable stream of leads coming into the business.

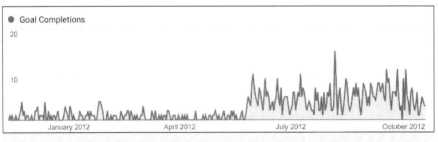

A screenshot of the rise in goal completions caused by launching the new lead generation website for a property management customer. [Captured using Google Analytics]

Very quickly they were also able to stop expensive advertising in local newspapers, Yellow Pages and several other areas which they'd hoped would work but weren't actually driving any revenue at all. This saving more than covered the cost of our fees, let alone the additional monthly revenue obtained from running all apartments at full capacity.

Our system was able to unveil what worked and what didn't. Giving us the incredible advantage of focusing on improving the advertising that did work and ditching the stuff that didn't. This is a luxury that many business owners don't have.

Over the course of the years that have since followed, our customer has always been able to let apartments quickly whenever they become available, sometimes within a matter of just a few hours. It wasn't long before our marketing system was the only form of marketing they used.

Providing an extra layer of stability to a business like this can seriously strengthen its position both at the time and into the future. Over the years, the business has been able to provide regular maintenance to apartments and health facilities including the swimming pool. They also extended the property with an additional 12 apartments, rebuilt the management office area for the onsite staff and successfully gained planning permission to build another similar building across the road.

Needless to say, our work and relationship continued to go from strength to strength with new ideas being tested and monitored on an ongoing basis. We were regularly invited to an annual VIP cricket event at Edgbaston Cricket Club for their most valued suppliers and partners, as a thank you for the hard work and results we were achieving over the years.

Discovering A Hidden Gem

Now and then in business and life, you notice something that you've not noticed before, yet it has been there all along. Well, that's exactly what happened to us.

In May 2017, we received our invites to attend that year's cricket event which happened to be the first ever day/night Test Match in England against the West Indies.

When the day arrived, I was excited to be representing our business at this year's event. As I walked into the hospitality suite, I expected to see the usual group of guests ranging from bank managers to building managers and furniture suppliers, but instead, I was surprised to see that the owners had invited their wives and family members. It turns out that the only supplier who had an invitation that year was us!

It didn't take too long before the personal "thank yous" started for the work that we'd completed on their behalf over the previous six years. It turns out that five shareholding directors had decided to sell the business for a significant 8-figure sum. It only really hit me at this very moment, just how integral the owners had viewed our work in the development and ultimately in the sale of their business for a value higher than they had initially hoped.

As I was leaving Edgbaston that evening, walking back to the car, I could not stop thinking about the difference we had made. What was it that we had really done for them? How had it been so effective? The answer was simple. We had systematically combined many individual components of internet marketing and got them working together in complete harmony.

We knuckled down and did the grunt work that many marketers find boring, and many designers and developers don't even know exists. We never went off in search of the latest trends or having our heads turned by new shiny objects. We implemented a proven local marketing system. The very same strategies and processes which form the basis of today's system, which is now stronger and more consistent than ever before.

CHAPTER 3

The Mission

A Mission To Change The Lives of Business Owners Around The World

Before we get into the details of our local marketing system and exactly how it can work for you, I'd like to explain to you why we've decided to share this with the world and not just keep it safely locked away solely for use with our high-level customers.

Like most business owners we started out on our own because of a 'jolt'. Usually, it's a particular circumstance that causes a business owner to get out of the comfort zone provided by having a job and take the leap of faith into the unknown world of running your own business.

Whether it's a bad a boss, redundancy, financial difficulty, unfulfillment in your career, there's usually some reason for taking that first step.

Like most new business owners, we started out providing the same services which we'd previously done in our job.

The big problem which this situation creates is that a web designer has only ever done the web designing, not the running of a business.

The short-term feeling was great. We were now our own boss. We called the shots, decided when we finished work or took holidays. We felt an immense sense of pride in the work we did and customers felt like close friends. These customers told their friends, and soon we had more satisfied customers, and things really started to get busy. If things carried on like this, we'd soon have the business empire of our dreams.

Whilst this all seems fantastic in the short-term, it does create problems a little later on, sometimes months or even years down the line. You quickly find that you only have so many hours in the day, and this business created for freedom gradually starts to feel more like a weight around your neck.

From the vast amount of entrepreneurs we meet and speak with, this pattern is, unfortunately, more common than you might expect and getting out of this situation requires a steely determination, a solid strategy and yet more hard work.

Making A Real Difference

We felt that we had more to give to a web design and digital marketing industry which had become rife with people promising the world and not being held accountable for the work they were doing.

Many businesses don't back up their promises with actual results, and we knew we could do better. I'm not saying that most people in this industry are charlatans and stealing your money, far from it. However many of them just don't get the results, and on the occasions when they do, it's more down to chance than planned execution.

Having set sail on our valiant journey, we soon found the path to be winding, hard to follow and peppered with difficult challenges along the way. From cash flow problems, management issues and the hugely painful experience of making hardworking staff redundant. Life became challenging, stressful and far from the freedom we'd hoped for.

After more than 7 years of trial and error, and some damn hard work, we're now in the fortunate position where the business is growing at the rate we'd hoped for all those years ago. For this we're grateful for some good fortune, meeting some fantastic people along the way, and above all the continued commitment from ourselves, our staff, our families and our loyal customers.

We feel if we can share this wisdom with other business owners and make their journey a tiny little bit easier and shorter, then that's precisely what we intend to do.

However, in early 2017, things in our business took an incredible turn for the worse. After a very short complaint with a pain in his side, Lee was devastatingly diagnosed with stage 4 bowel cancer which had also spread to his liver. Given only a 50% chance of surviving, it harrowingly put into perspective what's important in life, and just how precious each and every moment that each one of us has on this planet.

For the next 12 months, Lee underwent a series of excruciating operations and treatments that pushed him and his family to the extreme edge. With countless hospital appointments, love and support of his friends and family, a highly committed team of medical experts and an unbreakable desire to beat this cruel disease, Lee remained 100% focused and positive on his ability to win this fight.

For me, seeing one of my closest friends battle through this life-changing ordeal with such determination and positivity has been a real inspiration and one that I will never forget.

Thankfully, I'm delighted to say that Lee has defied the odds and has recently officially gone into remission meaning there are no more traces of cancer in his body. Whilst this is not yet 'all clear', it's a massive milestone achievement in this incredible journey.

Whilst remaining in constant contact with Lee, one of the driving factors behind keeping focused on his recovery was the work that we were doing in our business and the fact that we still have so much further to go in our dream for what we want to achieve.

The positive impact this has had on the business, is that we've never been more focused on our plan for Go Websites. In fact, it is one of the reasons, we've decided to write this book and share all of the details of our local marketing system with small business owners not just in the UK but all around the world.

Furthermore, we've also made it our mission to our customers to help them generate a collective total of one million leads over the coming years.

We sincerely hope that what you read in this book will help you not only to identify the best way to drive new customers into your business, but also give you the clear instructions to get started quickly.

CHAPTER 4

What Makes This System Different?

You might be thinking to yourself 'why hasn't my previous web designer implemented a system like this or at least even mentioned it?' Unfortunately, your designer or developer is not a marketer. It's not their fault; it's just what they've always known and been taught.

They are more focused on the appearance and creating a piece of artwork that either they or you really like the look of. They usually have little or no knowledge or interest in the age-old marketing concepts that have been proven to work for hundreds of years, regardless of the medium through which these messages are being told.

Although many people unknowingly go off in search of hiring a web designer, they actually need, whether they realise it or not, a skilled marketer who knows precisely how to generate a predictable stream of local leads.

Any successes these designers or developers may have had in terms of generating a return on investment (ROI), always comes down to either chance, or more likely their client understands these marketing techniques, and they are merely a vehicle for getting them implemented.

Before you start thinking I'm being overly critical of web designers, I can say this confidently, because I also started out as a designer/developer who thought in this very same way. I plied my trade in some of the UK's largest web agencies at the time and worked and met with hundreds of fellow designers, ALL of which, think in exactly the same way.

Even after starting our business and having no choice but to adjust my mindset, it still took me a long time to correct my thinking and allow myself to achieve great success in lead generation both online and in other marketing arenas.

Multi-Agency Approach

Another possibility is that you are currently using several agencies. Perhaps one who looks after your website, one who looks after your SEO and another who posts your social media. Whilst many business owners like the fact they are spreading the risk and not having one single company in control, it actually means there is no individual company or person accountable for ensuring more leads are coming in. There will be no desire or opportunity to share insights in order to improve all other components. The buck will be passed between all parties, and the focus will become more on delivering 'work product' than putting profit into your pocket.

DIY Website Builder

One of the most significant changes in recent years is the ease at which any member of the public can now build a website for themselves at an incredibly low cost, sometimes for free. Whilst this is a fantastic development, it also brings with it a considerable risk to your business. In order for this to work, the person building it also needs to be an experienced marketer. It's a similar case to the web designer; however, now the site won't even look as nice.

This situation creates a fantastic opportunity for your business as many of your competitors will be tempted to make their website themselves and make more marketing mistakes than ever before. This makes the information in this book even more lucrative for your mission to take a larger proportion of the available leads in your marketplace.

CHAPTER 5

The Website Is Dead

You're probably thinking, that is quite a dramatic claim, and you'd be right, but hear me out. We first need to define what a 'website' is, and why this approach is not going to work for you now, let alone in the future.

Whether you are currently in business, or just starting out, you will have no doubt figured out, or been told of the importance of having a website?

But why? Here are some popular reasons:

- Everybody has one these days
- Your competitors have one too
- As a business, people will expect you to have one
- It's an extension of your business card
- It would be nice to have a well designed professional website
- Your existing website is looking tired and old
- So people can see what services you offer

Although these are reasons for having a website developed, and some or many of them may be true, they are not reasons that should be important to you or your business. The real reason should be born from something more profound.

- Your business needs more customers or sales leads
- Maybe you need a higher calibre of customer, so that you can start earning the profit that you deserve and not just making ends meet?
- Maybe you want to expand the whole size of your operation?
- Alternatively, perhaps you're just simply running out of hours in your day, and you want to use the website to share useful information on your behalf

So what has the website done wrong?

A website or a web page is information which is hosted for the world to see on the Internet. So it's not technically 'websites' that I have a problem with, but more the process that most people go through to create one, along with their expectations of what it should do for their business.

When it comes to designing a new website, there seems to be a similar process that the vast majority of people seem to follow. What's worse is that because everyone does this, everyone assumes that this must be the right way to go about it.

The first thing which most business owners do is take a look at their competitors' websites to see what *they* are doing, choose one that they like the look of and then effectively copy it when building their own website. One of the first questions that most web designers ask is "Can you give me a list of websites that you like the look of".

You might copy their style and layout, the pages that they have in their navigation, the names of these pages, or even possibly talk about the same things they do, in the same kind of style.

This is a big mistake. If the majority of small businesses are struggling, then we can only assume that the majority is wrong in their thinking.

This process will pretty much always end up with a 'nice looking' (or at least in your opinion anyway) page, which fails to attract any new business just like the websites you've copied.

What ends up happening is most businesses wind up with very similar looking websites, with similar navigation structure, similar style of copywriting and a similar message.

So let's assume you now have your website live on the internet and you are waiting for the huge volume of visitors that are about to come crashing in like a wave.

Any time now…

You've told your family and friends to take a look. Perhaps they'll be able to spread the word for you?

Anyone?

Unfortunately, the realisation comes reasonably soon that this website isn't going to generate any business on its own. So you have two options, the first is to just write it off as a learning exercise and just carry on as usual, albeit a few thousand pounds out of pocket. Alternatively, you can try to figure out how you can get people to your website.

If you're going to get people to your website, and more importantly legitimate prospects, then you're going to need to get a stream of good quality website visitors, known as traffic.

This could be made up of:

- **Search engines** - People who are searching for your company name, or better yet, people who are looking for a company who provides the products and services you offer. Traffic can happen 'organically' appearing in the natural search results or can be paid for using the search engine's ad programme (more on these later).
- **Social media** - This could be people coming directly from Facebook, Twitter or any other social network.
- **Email marketing** - People who visit your website from a link in an email you sent personally or using email marketing software.
- **Website links** - Websites that link to your website as a useful resource.
- **Offline marketing** - People who manually type in your website address from your business cards, banners, flyers or even word of mouth.

All things considered, getting the website set up is the easy bit, getting good quality traffic is where many small businesses struggle. This is because it's going to require a significant investment in terms of money to get this completed on your behalf or even more so in time, if you're going to learn this yourself.

What happens now?

So let's just assume you get this far, and by the way, most small businesses don't, you would still expect to see a return from this investment. Sadly, although this may be enough for some businesses, it's often still not going to generate an adequate return for others. To help me explain why this is, take a look at the following diagram.

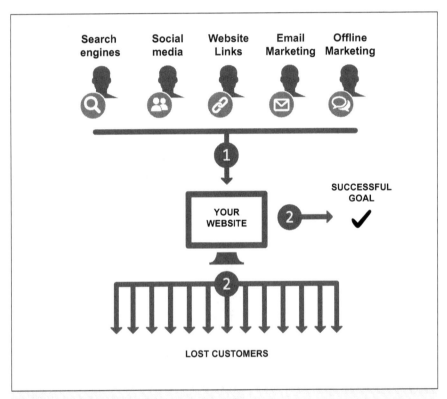

Diagram of traffic flow through a 'normal' website

As the traffic flows into your website, some of these people will take a look around, and some may submit an enquiry, make a phone call, or complete a web form (these are known as conversions or goals).

However, the sad reality is that most will just leave. They may have a look around, but eventually, they'll just leave without taking any action. The average website for a local business has a conversion rate (the percentage of people that complete an action such as filling out a form) of just 3%, this means a vast 97% of people that land on your website will, in fact, leave without taking any action whatsoever.

Now you might be thinking, well, why not just aim to increase the amount of traffic coming through in the first place? Yes, that would no doubt increase the number of conversions or goals proportionally, but don't forget that traffic in today's market comes at a premium. The problem you need to fix first is the 'hole in your bucket'.

So let's move on, and take a closer look at those people who didn't convert (i.e. make an enquiry, make a phone call or a purchase etc.).

There are many legitimate reasons for people leaving your site, many of them we can all relate to.

So with the exception of the people, who were in the wrong place, or have no need for your product or service, let's take a look at some of the reasons.

- They're just doing some research at this stage.
- They need a little more time to think about it - everybody is guilty of putting things off, especially when opening your wallet or purse is involved.
- They haven't quite got the budget yet.
- They're not sure if they can trust you yet - trust is usually built over time, and if they've only just landed on your website, it's understandable that they might not want to dive in head first.
- They still need to browse your competitor's website - many people like to shop around before committing.

No matter what the visitor's intention was, or whether they plan to come back in the future, there are now a million and one other things that will be competing for their attention and money. Will they ever come back? Statistically speaking, very few of them will do, you'll drop off their radar probably for good.

But don't despair!

This is where things get interesting...

CHAPTER 6

Systems = Success

Think for a moment about a particular task you might complete in your business on a regular basis. It could be something like producing a sales quotation for a new customer or signing off a completed project. How do you ensure that it gets completed exactly the same way each and every time? It's by using systems.

Every good business uses systems and processes, whether they are well-thought out, structured and written down or they are stored in the owner's head and passed on verbally. So when I say systems or processes, I'm simply talking about a pre-agreed 'way of doing things around here'.

The aim of your systems are to help you and your team to complete jobs consistently on a regular basis. These tasks could include how you provide a quote, set up your work environment, manage your bookkeeping, quality control check your projects, report issues, manage staff performance reviews or any other tasks you might undertake during the day to day running of your company.

These systems may not be perfect from day one, but with the help of continually making small adjustments and tweaks, you will soon have things running like clockwork and much more predictably.

In fact, without these systems, it can be very difficult to ensure that important tasks are completed on time, to consistently high standards, or to ensure that every customer gets the same high level of service on every project. Working without a clear set of instructions can be erratic, tiring, stressful and ultimately very expensive.

So why is it then that most businesses seem to miss this very fact when addressing their sales and marketing? The majority of small businesses seem to 'hope' that work comes from networking events, random promotions, word of mouth referrals, or via their website. If you rely on random chance to bring in your new sales, you will no doubt also find it to be very erratic, tiring, stressful and expensive in your life.

The point I'm making is that success in marketing, just like in business, is about getting the foundations in place and keeping a close eye on them to make sure they are working. This is exactly what you're going to learn in the coming chapters.

It's time to stop thinking about your marketing in terms of individual and unconnected campaigns that have no bearing on each other, and more about a series of interconnected components that when working in harmony, will produce predictable and pleasing results.

Imagine what this would bring to your business if you could accurately predict the number of new customers and revenue coming into your business over the coming months. Furthermore, the benefit of being able to proactively identify problems as soon as they begin to arise, not when it's too late to do anything about it.

I'd like to introduce you to the local marketing system. This is the antidote to the plain old-fashioned website. This is the ultimate system for maximising the number of local leads that your business is able to generate consistently .

You may have heard people tell you about the 3 seconds (or clicks) rule. You have 3 seconds of your prospect's time, and if they don't find what they are looking for, they will move on. Although I don't necessarily buy into the *exactly* 3 seconds or clicks things, I do feel the principle is certainly true. You don't have much time at all. The name of the game is to get and hold your readers' attention.

The Go Websites approach gives you one big advantage; it buys you time. It means that if a conclusive buying decision isn't reached in the first few seconds (which it most likely won't be), then you still have a marketing system in place to continue the sales process.

Just because a prospect says they are not going to buy today, it doesn't mean they're not going to buy EVER. In fact, put yourself in this situation and think of a purchase you've made in the past few months, did you immediately decide to buy the very first time you interacted with the brand? The majority of people don't.

So I'd like you to think of the marketing system as a multi-point system or process that you can follow to help nurture those prospects by demonstrating how you can help them and building good rapport and trust over time. So that when the time comes, you are in position ready to help them take action.

Understanding Your Marketing System

As I've already mentioned, the local marketing system is made up of 10 individual steps. As you can see from the diagram on page 26, the 10 steps fall into 4 phases which represent the lifecycle of a new prospect or customer.

All of these steps are extremely important, and although they may have a positive impact if used alone, combining all of the 10-steps in order will compound the effect, and it's here where the magic begins to happen.

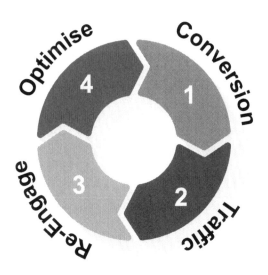

Phases Of The Cycle

1. <u>Conversion</u> - This phase is about building something that compels people to take action when they see your marketing. Things that will have an impact on this stage are the way your web pages are structured and what you say to the prospect to build trust and confidence to take action.
2. <u>Traffic</u> - This is the phase where we drive the right people through to your website to see your sales message.
3. <u>Re-Engagement</u> - These are the activities which are conducted after your visitor has stopped viewing your website and designed to bring them back for a further opportunity to take action.
4. <u>Optimisation</u> - This phase is designed to provide ongoing improvements to all components of your system to ensure that your performance keeps on getting better.

In comparison to a standard website

In order to explain how each of these components work, we'll start by overlaying this into the previous diagram outlined for a standard website.

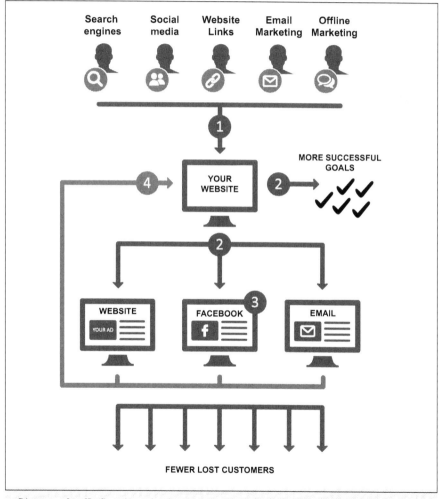

Diagram of traffic flow through a local marketing system

As you can see, each of the ten steps has its place in the overall cycle. Before we dig deeper into each step, I'd first like to explain from a top-level perspective exactly how they all work.

The first component that we'll cover in the conversion phase will be **step 1. The Message**. The message is the step where we construct a powerful sales argument which is designed to stop your prospect in their tracks and make them pay attention to what you're saying. The message should be unique and help to position your business to stand apart from other generic companies with whom you are competing. This message can then lead to the creation of your website, adverts, blogs, social media content and more.

In the next stage, your sales message should be applied to **step 2. Lead Generation Website**. A carefully structured web page which incorporates proven best practices for encouraging people to take action, often ignoring the usual design fads and trends that most designers would love you to follow.

When visitors come through to your website, they are attracted using the steps which make up the traffic phases of your system. These traffic sources offer a wide range of ways to get the right people to your site.

Step 3. Google Ads is the fast acting way to get your website to the top of the search engine for your most profitable keywords and start the process of driving traffic straight away.

Step 4. SEO (Search engine optimisation) is supportive to your Google Ads and allows you to take the keywords that are working there, and transfer to build strong natural rankings in Google's 'most trusted' organic search results.

Step 5. Social Media channels such as Facebook and Twitter will be used to carefully build relationships with your fans and ultimately drive people back through to your website along the way.

Step 6. Blogging will help to position you as an expert in front of your prospects with detailed and well-researched content. This work will also help to drive more customers who are looking to learn about your subject matter.

Unfortunately, even the most successful websites will not be able to catch everyone. In fact, the majority of visitors will leave without taking any further action. It's the re-engagement phase where your local marketing system will start to pull away from the pack. Where most websites stop at this point, we have more opportunity to reach your prospects on multiple occasions, hopefully persuading a small number of these otherwise 'lost' visitors to take action.

The first tool we will use is **step 7. Facebook Ads**. Facebook is the largest and most used social network in the world, so is a great place to reach your visitors once again. Visitors to your website are tracked by Facebook, allowing you to show your ads only to people who have recently shown interest.

Further to this, we can also use **step 8. Remarketing** to show your eye-catching adverts to recently interested prospects whilst they browse millions of other websites including Amazon, eBay and YouTube. Many people describe the action of the adverts as 'following them around on the web'. They are a great way to continue sharing your message and capture a further number of people who procrastinated first time around.

Finally, in the re-engagement phase, we have **step 9. Automated Follow-Up**. This is where people who have provided their contact information either as part of an initial enquiry or in exchange for useful free information, can be emailed with interesting educational and sales information at regular intervals over the coming weeks and months. This helps to keep in the minds of your prospects and maximise the number of people who decide to purchase from you.

The last phase and arguably the most important stage that nearly all web designers and marketers will miss, the Optimise phase. The process of continually optimising and testing your local marketing system in order to ensure it gets better with age. The secrets of this process are mapped out in **step 10. Testing & Optimisation**.

Having now discovered an overview of how these work, it's now time to drill into each aspect to find out exactly why they work and more importantly the steps you can take to implement them into your business with immediate effect.

CHAPTER 7

Conversion

Step 1. Your Message

When someone views your web page, they make a decision to either get in touch or click back to where they came from. What makes them leave their contact details can depend on many reasons. Some of these are completely out of your control, however, there are a number of proven strategies that will help to maximise the number of people who do take action.

The first stage in our system is not only one of the most important, but it is also one of the most overlooked by business owners, therefore a real chance for you to get an advantage over your competitors. Your 'message', when put simply, is what you choose to say to your customer when they are in front of you (e.g. on your website). This message should help to convince the prospect of what makes your offering different to all others and how they will benefit from choosing your products over anyone else's. This message can then be conveyed at any given opportunity through written text, videos or even diagrams and images.

Take a look at the following diagram on page 32. It describes each of the components of an advertising campaign. The 3 components are message, market and media.

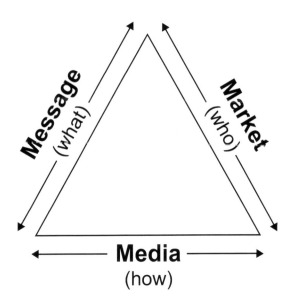

- **Message (What)** - This is what you offer, how it differs from other options available and what is it that makes your business, products and promotions different from other alternatives.
- **Market (Who)** - This is the group of people that your message will be shown to.
- **Media (How)** - This is how your message will reach your market, the channels through which the message will be delivered, examples could include your website, a newspaper advert, social media, word of mouth, etc.

When it comes to doing any form of advertising, most business owners start with the media that they are going to use, as it represents the most exciting part of the project for them. Let's build a website, let's run some Facebook ads, let's get a stand at an exhibition. All of this happens before they've even started to think about just what it is they are going to say, and what makes them stand apart from the crowd.

It really doesn't matter how much traffic you drive into your website if your message doesn't provide a compelling reason for your prospect to take action then you'll be seriously missing out when it comes to the number of visitors that turn into enquiries.

In this chapter, we will be covering the following six areas of building the perfect message for your business.

1. Products and services
2. Customer profiling
3. USP
4. Lead magnet
5. Brand personality
6. Copywriting tips

Section 1 - Products and Services

In this section I'd like you to take a close look at the products and services that you are currently offering, or perhaps would like to offer in the future. It's fair to say that not all products are born equal, and some may be easier to sell or perhaps some may cause you more stress than others. This exercise is designed to help you establish a clear priority and help you to focus your efforts into the most profitable areas of your business.

Start by listing each of your key products or services in a table like the one drawn below. If you do have lots, then you might want to consider grouping them into categories or perhaps just focusing on the ones that you deem to be most important in achieving the long-term goals of the business.

Product or service	Priority

Once you've done that, I'd like you to read the list of questions below and mark an asterisk (*) next to the product or service which you feel is most suited as the answer. This helps to visualise which products are your company's highest priority.

- What does your company do best?
- Which services/products are your current biggest sellers?
- Which services/products do you want to be your biggest sellers?

- Which services/products have the least competitors?
- Which services/products make the most profit?
- Which services/products can be turned around quickly?
- Which services/products cause the least strain on customer service?
- Which services/products will lead to more sales or ongoing repeat business?

Tip: One thing that always helps to put things into perspective quickly is to imagine your phone is ringing in your business. It's someone making an enquiry or looking to buy. If you could choose the product or service which they are calling about, what would it be and why?

Once you've given this some thought, I'd then like you to fill out the priority column. This again helps you to prioritise the products and services which will help you to achieve your business goals.

You may not spot the benefit in doing this at first, but please proceed as there are a number of reasons this task is required for building your system. Firstly, we strongly believe in focusing the majority of your effort on the most effective areas. This means that you can focus on your best products first, and as scary as it may seem, actually stop wasting your time on your worst products.

A while back when we completed this task ourselves, we identified that the management of email mailboxes for our customers was one of the biggest stresses on our support team, yet at the same time, it was an area in which we were making the least profit (in fact it was losing us money). We didn't take much persuading to look for alternative solutions. We now use recommended partners who love email and are better equipped with the expertise and support teams to help our customers out. It's a win-win situation for all parties.

Further to this, the data that you establish in this exercise will be of critical importance when it comes to researching search engine keywords in later stages.

Section 2: Your Customers

Next time you are browsing a small business website, take a look at what they talk about. Most businesses are only talking about themselves and using their marketing as an opportunity to massage their own ego.

Let's shift the focus from thinking about you and your business to thinking about your customers and their needs. It's what you discover here that will form the foundation of what you are going to talk about in your sales message.

Customer Profiling

Customer profiling involves taking each separate type of customer that your business works with and gaining a deeper understanding about what makes them tick. Now you might be thinking that you couldn't possibly do this as you have too many customers and all of them are different. In which case you will need to start to look at customer groups, and more importantly focus only on the customer groups which you would deem to be the most valuable to your business objectives. For example, if your company sells to both businesses and consumers, you may wish to include both of these groups as separate customer types. If required, you can always repeat this process for up to 3-5 different customer profiles.

There are five key questions to answer for each customer profile. Remember to answer these in the context of your products and services, and the more detail you can go into, the better understanding you will have of their emotional needs:

1. Describe the customer in terms of their age, gender, income, likes, dislikes etc.
2. What is their biggest problem? What is keeping them awake at night?
3. What is their biggest desire? Remember this is in context of your products and services.
4. How will their life be different when they buy from you?
5. What will it cost them if they don't buy your product?

The information that you establish during this exercise will be invaluable when it comes to writing powerful copy. Not only will you be able to talk directly to the needs of the customer, but you'll also be able to resonate with their biggest hopes and desires for life once they've purchased from you.

A great example of this would be with a typical tradesperson, for example, a builder. The typical building company website may assume that people want to know about:

- Where they are based
- How good they are at building
- How long they've been doing it for
- All of the different types of project they could potentially build for you

These points are all valid, but if you speak to the customer who is looking to hire a builder they might have concerns about:

- Will they show up when they say they will
- Will the project overrun?
- Will there be hidden costs that I might have to pay?
- Will this affect my family being able to live in the house?
- Can I trust this person?
- Will they use bad language in front of my children?
- Will they run off with my money?

Identifying these emotional points will literally reveal a secret path to developing a message which truly connects with what is being said in your customer's head. Constructing a message around these points will help you to stand apart from the crowd.

Tip: If you are unsure of this information, or would just like to reinforce what you believe to be true, then the single most effective thing to do is to speak to real customers and prospects. Ask existing customers by emailing them, building an online survey or just picking up the phone. The insight received using this process will help to better serve other customers in their position.

Section 3: Unique Selling Proposition

It's now time to build a marketing message that is going to resonate with your customer in such a way that they feel almost compelled to do business with you. One of the quickest ways to achieve this is to make yourself stand out from the competition with a powerful unique selling proposition (USP).

Whether it's something that you offer which is different to everyone else, or whether you've made a conscious effort not to do the annoying things which your competitors do, this short statement can do great things for your marketing.

A USP should be short and concise and clearly describe your proposition in order to capture the reader's interest. This is not the same thing as a tagline or a slogan (although it can be used to replace both of these.)

It's something about your business which they can instantly connect with and even pass on to their friends when they are talking about your brand.

When coming up with a USP you really should be looking to answer the question, *"Why should I choose to do business with you over every other option available?"*. If your answer doesn't stop them in their tracks, then it's probably not focused strongly enough on their immediate needs.

We've done a lot of work with helping business owners to develop a unique selling proposition, and one of the most common mistakes is not thinking big enough. If I were to ask 100 businesses what separates them from the competition, the majority would say, "excellent customer service", "good quality", "affordable prices" etc. This is nowhere near as compelling, specific or unique enough to get your prospects to take note.

This process is not a 2-minute job and may require several attempts and edits before you actually come up with something genuinely powerful. Answer the following questions to get started with building your USP.

1) Use these questions to help build your USP:

1. What do you do that's great - better than all other competitors?
2. How does this 'great' thing benefit your target market?
3. Can your USP specifically identify your target market?
4. Is there an opportunity gap/void in the marketplace that you can fill?
5. Can you offer a great guarantee?
6. What can you fix that people hate?
7. Can what you do be delivered quickly or within a certain time frame?

Here's a couple of examples of powerful USP's which can help to provide inspiration to get you started.

Example 1: Domino's Pizza's Classic USP
"Fresh, Hot Pizza Delivered In 30 Minutes Or Less Or It's FREE"

When starting out, Domino's Founder, Tom Monaghan, came up with a USP which quite simply changed the trajectory of his business in a very short amount of time and became the driving force behind his company experiencing incredibly fast growth.

As a student himself, Tom's first takeaway pizza stores were situated near university campuses. The big problem that he was able to identify is that students had no means, desire or in some cases weren't in any fit state to go out and get food. They wanted carbs, and they wanted them quickly. That's where Domino's were able to provide a solution. If you pay careful attention, there is no mention of great tasting pizza, it's simply fresh and hot, and if it's not there in 30 minutes, you don't have to pay a single penny.

This foundation was incredibly successful. It was only when the business scaled and could no longer logistically guarantee they could reach everywhere in 30 minutes, that they discontinued its use.

Example 2: Go Websites

"At Least Double Your Local Leads In 90 Days Or Your Money-Back - 100% Guaranteed"

For the second example, I would like to show you how we've been able to create our USP at Go Websites. Starting out as a traditional website design and internet marketing company, we looked at what our best customers desired most. It was to significantly increase the number of high quality leads coming into their business. Further to this, many people have had bad experiences with marketing companies from which either the agency they hired didn't deliver on their promise, or were simply unable to achieve the desired results.

With such a groundbreaking perspective, we've been able to restructure our business to become so focused on the goals of our customers and in turn focus solely on delivering our unique 10-part system. By retaining full control of all 10 marketing components, we can legitimately guarantee to get this working and subsequently take 100% of the risk in the relationship.

2) Test Your USP

As with all components of your local marketing system the best way to see what works and what doesn't, is to simply test it and gain evidence from real customers. A simple way to test your USP will be to use it on your website and see how it performs. Test different USP variations to see which one performs best with your actual target market.

Section 4: Your Offer

When creating a powerful message to put in front of your customers, you simply must have a compelling reason to take action (call to action) right away. Just to be clear, when I talk about an 'offer', I'm not referring specifically to a promotion or a discounted price, but instead a general term for 'your reason to get in touch now'.

Your 'offer' can be as much as 50% of the success or failure of your lead generation campaign, so it's critical that you invest an adequate amount of time into making sure it is both powerful and related to the exact needs of the customer.

If you take the typical website, the only opportunity you might be given to get in touch will be a page on their site called 'Contact Us'. This is usually a page where the business displays their contact information and possibly a form which can be used to send an enquiry.

Whilst a contact page is critical for your business, as far as an offer goes, it's pretty weak, and certainly won't be sending any ripples through your marketplace any time soon.

1) Offer Ideas / Lead Magnets

Here is a list of items which you might want to consider when coming up with an offer

i) **Remove Risk** - Can you do anything for your customer without obligation? This method works on the basis of proving you can help someone *by actually helping them*. Making something free is a fantastic way to remove any resistance towards getting in touch. With this approach, it's critical that the experience your customer receives during this trial is capable of encouraging them to purchase further from you.

Examples include:
- A free consultation
- A free appraisal
- A free taster session
- A free trial period

ii) **Useful Information** - Can you put together any useful information that can help a potential customer to make a decision or resolve a problem? These guides are often called lead magnets as they are a great way to attract leads.

Information is a great way to attract people who still need educating/convincing of potential solutions before going ahead. A lead generation magnet (or lead magnet) is an irresistible offer of something valuable (and usually free) to be given to your prospect in exchange for their contact information.

Depending on the nature of your business or requirements, you could request name, email address, physical address, contact numbers as well as other information.

Examples include:
- Buyers guide for your products or services
- Free ebook or guide
- Physical book
- Automated email series
- Webinar (online presentation)
- Video.

iii) **Promotions** - Promotions are a great way to attract people who are ready to buy and encourage them to take action with immediate effect. Whilst you may or may not want to discount your main products or services, there are often ways to give promotional rates for other aspects of your business.

Examples include:
- Introductory discount offer
- Discount coupons/vouchers
- Free bonus with every enquiry or order placed

2) Name Your Offer

As simple as it may sound, giving your offer a name can make it feel like a 'real thing' and increase its perceived value, making it easy to share and talk about. Here are a few example names to get you started.

- The Ultimate Boiler Repair Gift
- Step-By-Step Back-Pain Removal Formula
- New Kitchen Design Toolkit
- Advanced Bookkeeping System

3) Test Your Offer Names

The only way to see if your offer resonates with your target market is to actually test it with real-life prospects and see which one gets the best response.

Section 5: Defining Your Brand Personality & Style

When it comes to ensuring that your customers are left with a lasting impression, it's important to define a clear personality for your business. So whether your customers come into contact with you via an email, your website or even over the phone, there is a consistency that they can immediately relate to in the way that you are seen to communicate.

By completing this exercise, you will be able to establish a code of ethics and a tone of voice, which can then be easily adopted by anyone acting within or on behalf of your business. The most effective way to visualise this is to think of your business as a human being.

Decide how this person would be perceived by others and the personality traits they would possess. It's always interesting to see how closely your desired personality reflects that of how your business is actually perceived at this moment in time.

Don't forget; you have already identified your ideal customers, so be sure that your tone and voice is aligned with these customer profiles.

Take a look at the list of words on page 43. Write a number next to each item to prioritise which personality traits and tones of voice you feel are most suitable for your communications. 1 being the most important, 2 being second etc.

Personality Traits:

- Friendly
- Trustworthy
- Innovative
- Approachable
- Relaxed
- Precise

- Fun-loving
- Helpful
- Dependable
- Caring/kind
- Optimistic
- Discreet

Tone Of Voice:

- Motivational
- Polite
- Friendly
- Professional
- Sympathetic
- Proactive

- Excited/energetic
- Respectful
- Assertive
- Calm
- Humorous
- Non-technical

Design, Images and Styles

So here we are in the final section of developing a powerful message. This is coincidentally the part where most other website designers start (and sometimes also finish). What type of colours, photos and styles are to be used to get your message across?

Now the most amazing thing about this system is that this part should really complete itself. This is because you already know who your customer is, what they value and how best to communicate it. You should focus solely on selecting images, photos, colours, styles and overall pricing and positioning that is best suited to them, and not your own personal taste.

I'll never forget the time that I produced a design for a customer, and I was desperately excited to be unveiling it to him. You can imagine my horror when he proclaimed "I don't like it! I'm a huge Liverpool fan, so it has got to be red".

Don't treat your marketing like it's going to be hung up in your living room. Treat it like the business tool that it is, and judge it by how much it brings you in revenue, not how much you like the look of it.

Section 6: Copywriting Tips

I think it's really important that I first explain why it is that so many people struggle to write good marketing copy and also alert you to the common mistakes that most small businesses seem to make and how to avoid them.

Overcoming The Curse Of Knowledge

The curse of knowledge is a phrase which basically describes a situation where you know so much about a particular subject that you can't imagine what it would be like to not have this knowledge. You become unable to talk about the subject in a way that somebody who isn't an expert can understand. If this happens when you're talking to potential customers, it's likely that you could overwhelm, confuse or even alienate them. In a face to face situation, a puzzled look on someone's face will be enough to provide an indication, but when writing the copy for your website, it's much harder to spot it.

Now, this is something that we all do, something that we'll all continue to do, so follow these steps to make sure that it doesn't catch you out in the future.

- **Know your audience** - The more you get to know them, the more you'll understand which concepts work and which don't, and if you do have to use technical terms, be sure to explain them clearly before moving on.
- **Get a second opinion** - If you think it all makes sense, but you're not sure, then ask a friend or an actual customer just to take a look over it. Their feed-back will give you valuable insight.
- **Use stories** - Stories are a great way to keep your customers attention, and often help to explain the benefits of your products in a way that your customer will relate to.

The 5 Copywriting Mistakes That Small Businesses Just Can't Stop Making

When you start to think more about marketing you start to notice it literally everywhere.

For me, I end up spending hours analysing every single bit that I see, whether it's browsing the web, flicking through a newspaper or even just reading a menu when I'm at a restaurant with my wife.

It's almost unbelievable how often I see the same mistakes crop up over and over again and I'm going to share them with you in a moment.

Before I do, I just want to be clear that I'm not having a go. I understand that most small businesses are just unaware they are making these mistakes. They're not marketing experts, they don't want to be, they're experts at what they love doing. That said, unfortunately for them, they live in a competitive world, and this is your opportunity to get an advantage.

Mistake #1: Self Focus

Now to us, our businesses are really important, but to our customers, their priority is themselves. So hoping to grab the attention of your customers with an impressive 'about us' style statement won't allow the customer to clearly understand how you can actually help them.

A much more effective approach would be to start by relating to a problem that they have and sharing with them how you've helped people just like them to overcome it.

Mistake #2: Corporate Speak

When your website or marketing copy reads like it was written by a huge corporate organisation, it doesn't make you sound approachable. Bearing in mind that people actually buy from people, they'll probably like the fact that you are a small, approachable business, as you'll be more likely to understand their problems. What's more, if you haven't noticed this already, then keep an eye out, because these big corporations (that everybody is trying to sound like), are actually themselves working at personalising their own approach rather than being seen as a faceless organisation.

Mistake #3: Carpet Bombing

This is derived from warplanes that would drop bombs on everything in order to ensure that they hit the target. I'm not saying to look at your customers as enemy targets, but merely to illustrate that you'll need a lot of bombs for this approach to be successful. Marketing is the same, and as a small businesses you need to make sure that your marketing budget is spent thriftily. This means not focusing on generic advertising which tries to appeal to everybody, but instead being laser targeted on your ideal customer profile only.

Not all customers are born equal, so it's better to know the ones you like the most and try to talk to them directly.

Mistake #4: Features Instead Of Benefits

Another major mistake often made is focusing your copywriting on features instead of benefits. A feature is a tangible thing which your customer will take home, whereas the benefit is the emotional payoff they will receive when using the product.

Benefits are the true reason why people decide to part company with their cash. Here are some examples to explain this further:

- **A feature is an emergency boiler repair service**; the benefit is the customer's home being returned to a warm, comfortable and safe environment within a short period of time.
- **A feature is a house extension service**; the benefit is the customer being able to have a spacious office to work from home and therefore more time to spend with their children.
- **A feature is a tyre replacement service**; the benefit is the customer being able to rest assured knowing their motor vehicle is now safe on the roads.

Mistake #5: Don't Add Proof

What other people say about your business is infinitely more believable than what you say yourself. Most website copywriters seriously underestimate the power of adding proof to what they are saying. Proof could come in the form of testimonials, reviews, before and after photos, statistics, awards, and much more.

So just to recap, you will create better marketing messages if you:

- Focus on your customer's needs not your own
- Be seen as a human and not trying to sound like a corporation
- Be specific about whom you are speaking to
- Focus on benefit and not features
- Add lots of proof to your copywriting

CHAPTER 8

Conversion

Step 2. Lead Generation Website

Now we have our sales message in place, we can start to take a closer look at step 2 of the system, your Lead Generation Website.

The prospect of building a new website can be one of the more exciting projects a business can embark on. However it's no longer enough to just own a website or to have a nice looking website, it's more important than ever to construct a website that you can depend on when it comes to driving new sales leads into your business.

I have been building websites for businesses of all sizes since the late 90's, so we've had a lot of real-life experience in establishing what works and what doesn't. You probably won't be surprised to hear that following the latest design fads and trends rarely seems to bear any fruit when it comes to generating new leads for your business.

What works consistently well is to identify and appeal to the hopes, dreams and fears of your target market and create a powerful and emotive sales message that resonates with your target customer, and gives them a compelling reason to take action right away.

This type of website is called a Lead Generation Website. It will act as a starting point which can then be systematically tested and continually improved so that you can generate more leads tomorrow than you did today.

What Is A Lead Generation Website?

The vast majority of UK businesses currently own a website of some sort, whether it was designed professionally or created by themselves. As we've already described, the problem with most websites is that they are designed to look pretty. They are not designed to be as effective as possible when it comes to generating profit.

3 Critical Components Of Lead Generation Website Design

Building successful websites requires three important disciplines. It's only by carefully considering each of these areas that we can create a website which is capable of producing results.

Marketing

The most important component and the most often overlooked are the marketing techniques involved in constructing your page.

Local business websites are simply marketing tools created to attract, educate and persuade prospects to choose your products and services over one of your competitors.

Now that you have your sales message, your key website pages should use headlines, copywriting, offers and your USP to create a compelling reason to take action right away.

Design

Design is often the starting point for most web designers, however for maximum success, the design process should only commence once the marketing message has been established.

It's only once you have a powerful sales message that you will know exactly how everything should look and feel.

Once you have a clear marketing message, the design process will support and enhance those messages with a professional feel and help to give an excellent and trustworthy first impression to your potential customers.

Development

Development is the term for the 'building' or coding of the website. The process of building your website should only commence once you are completely happy with your designs and feel they effectively get across your marketing message.

The way that your website is coded is important to the success of your project.

Although the code is behind the scenes and hidden to the user, it still determines important factors, including how it works on different devices, how easy it is to update in the future and how fast the page loads.

The Anatomy Of A Lead Generation Website

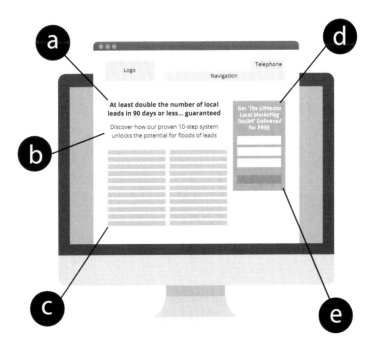

a) Attention grabbing headline

The most important element of any web page is the initial headline which the viewer is able to read. This is responsible for the decision to read on or go back to Google. The headline should concisely describe the key benefits of the sales message in one powerful sentence.

b) Intriguing supporting headline (Sub-headline)

If the headline has captured the reader's attention, the aim of the sub-headline is to plant enough intrigue that the reader feels compelled to keep on reading.

c) Compelling copywriting

The main body of the content should aim to complete the job started by the headline and sub-headline. It should help to portray all of the unique reasons why the reader should choose your business over any competitors, build trust in your business, help to overcome potential objections and ultimately describe the next steps of action.

d) Irresistible call to action
If you're expecting your readers to get in touch, then it's important to give them a compelling reason to do so now. Where most businesses stop at 'Get In Touch' or 'Contact Us' you should consider using an attractive lead magnet such as a free trial, free consultation, free gift pack or special offer.

e) Data capture form
Finally, all website pages should have a built-in web form so that your visitors can leave their contact information quickly and easily.

Landing Pages

One of the best ways to ensure that the viewer can decide on your offer quickly is to ensure that the page on which they have landed (landing page), contains content which is extremely relevant to what they typed into a search engine or the ad which they just clicked on.

It's important to be able to quickly produce new pages where the content can be slightly adjusted to be a perfect match for your reader. The more closely related a page's content is to your reader's search query, the higher the conversion rate of the page is likely to be.

Clarity Over Cleverness

One of the biggest mistakes made by even the most experienced of web designers is trying to be too clever with your marketing. It could be using headlines which require the customer to think too deeply. It could be using fancy sliders and visual effects, which might look impressive to other web designers and may help them to win design awards, but are not as good at helping the customer get a solution to their problem. Always favour clarity in every situation, after all 'a confused customer does nothing'.

Page Speed

One of the least mentioned aspects of good quality website design when it comes to generating more leads for your business is page speed. The longer it takes for your page to load on the user's screen, the exponentially higher the damage on your conversion rate. Ensure your website is built using the latest coding techniques as these are designed to render quickly on the user's browser rather than waiting for large images and files to be downloaded.

Mobile First

The shift in the use of mobile devices when browsing the web means that in some markets, desktop users are almost a thing of the past. Since the introduction of mobile devices, Google has always ordered (indexed) it's search results for mobile users separately from those using a desktop. In 2018 Google has finally decided to make the desktop index redundant from updates in order to solely focus its future on mobile devices. This means it's no longer enough for your website to be mobile compatible, your whole experience should be designed and developed from a mobile-first perspective.

Platform

Choosing a platform on which to build your website can be critical to the success of your lead generation activities. If there's one thing we've become pretty good at, it's recognising that what works is not often what you might expect. In fact, the only way to ensure that your marketing performs at it's best is to test regularly.

For this reason alone, I would wholeheartedly recommend that you ensure that you personally have the capability to edit and duplicate pages quickly using a CRM (Content Management System). We would recommend Wordpress given its vast library of third-party plugins, its performance and its ease of use for both developers and website administrators alike.

With everything in place to convert prospects into paying customers, now is the time to discover the best methods for finding the right people to see your message in the *traffic* phase.

CHAPTER 9

Traffic
Step 3. Google Ads

When it comes to generating more local leads for your business, I'm sure I don't need to explain the importance of appearing high in search engines, especially when those searchers are looking for your products and services. However, many business owners are unaware of the potential benefits of achieving this through the Google Ads advertising programme.

Google Ads (formerly known as Google AdWords) is without a doubt one of the best ways to quickly and efficiently generate great quality traffic for your local marketing system. Companies that get these campaigns working will often cite Google Ads as the most valuable aspect of their lead generation due to its speed, consistency and reliability.

Google Ads is a skill that many people talk about or have dabbled in, yet far fewer have actually mastered it or even got it working. If you've tried Google Ads before, you'll know first hand how difficult it is to learn all of the technical functions and settings just to get a campaign started.

It's very easy to make tiny mistakes which can have a devastating effect and burn away your entire budget.

What's more, with the continued growth of online marketing and the need to squeeze every last drop out of your marketing budget, Google Ads is getting even more competitive than ever before.

One of the biggest reasons for our success is that we've invested our own time and money. We've invested good pound after bad of our own money into making big mistakes and finding major breakthroughs. It's this learning which has paved the way for the techniques which you'll discover in this chapter.

What Is Google Ads?

Google Ads is the single biggest innovation when it comes to search engine marketing since search engines themselves. Google Ads is a robust advertising platform first launched in the year 2000, which allows advertisers to place ads for their products and services in some of the most prominent positions right at the top of all other search results.

The basic concept allows ads to be displayed when a searcher enters certain keywords or key phrases into the search engine. The advertiser gets charged for this advert if the user clicks on the ad; this model is commonly known as pay-per-click (PPC).

Advertisers compete with each other by controlling many factors such as how much they are prepared to pay for each click, how relevant their advert and web page is to the original search term and how well their ad performs.

Given that Google Ads is Google's most profitable revenue stream, it's easy to see why ad positioning is increasingly favourable over the organic listings offered by the SEO part of your marketing system.

Types Of Search Results

When it comes to typing your keywords or key phrases into Google, you'll notice there are a number of different types of results shown on the results page. For businesses looking for more local customers, ads commonly fall into two types.

Search Ads

Search ads are one of the most common adverts and usually appear at the top of the page above all other results as well as at the bottom, just before you move to the next page.

These ads are made up of components such as headlines, descriptions, links, click to call buttons, locations and even company reviews.

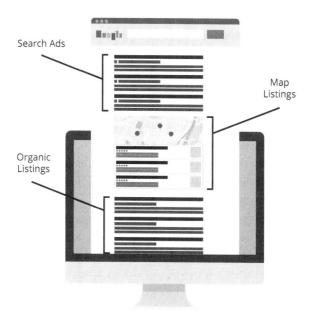

Search ads are positioned at the very top of the search results page in Google. Map listings and organic listings are covered in the SEO step (chapter 10).

Display Ads

Google's display network (GDN) allows you to show your adverts on millions of other websites around the world. This includes some of the world's largest websites such as eBay, Amazon, YouTube and many more.

This is most commonly used for Google Remarketing which is covered in the Remarketing section of your local marketing system which we'll come to a little later on.

Benefits Of Google Ads

- **Ready to buy traffic** - Like with all traffic from search engines, Google Ads allows you to get your products in front of people who are looking to buy them at that very moment in time. This traffic is not only the easiest to sell to, but also provides the fastest return on your investment.

- **Adverts live within minutes** - Possibly the fastest route to generating traffic available in the world. Once your ads are set to live and approved by Google, you can be receiving clicks and potentially enquiries and sales within minutes.

- **Test your marketing message** - With the speed at which your adverts can be set live, Google Ads is a great way to test your marketing messages and landing pages before commencing with a longer-term strategy provided by SEO.

- **The best possible position of your listing** - Ads are displayed before any organic listings, making this the best possible way to get your website seen before anyone else's.

- **Consistent results year on year** - Once your Google Ads campaign has been optimised and tested, it allows for extremely consistent results.

- **Fully trackable return on investment** - The robust Google Ads platform provides a wealth of data to ensure that you can see exactly what return on investment (ROI) is being achieved through your campaign.

Getting Started With Google Ads

Structuring Your Campaign

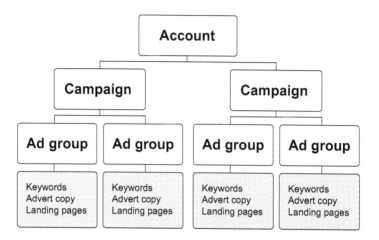

Illustration of how a Google Ads account is structured

Campaigns: Campaigns are a top-level way of grouping your ads in order to structure and organise them. Some settings are configured at campaign level, such as daily budget and location targeting. We predominantly recommend using campaigns for grouping products or services, locations, niches and high performing keywords.

Ad groups: Ad groups are subgroups which sit within each campaign. They are best used for maintaining a structured approach for ads and holding closely related groups of keywords.

Ads: Ads are the copywriting which the user will see on the search results page. The best approach for ads is to have them closely related to the keywords which are being used so that they are always relevant to exactly what is being searched for.

Landing pages: Each of your adverts will allow you to link through to a page on your website. This page is known as the landing page and will be of critical importance when it comes to increasing the number of leads your campaign generates.

Keyword Research

Keywords or key phrases are words entered by potential customers when they use Google to search for businesses which offer given products or services. Many keywords have different levels of usage and intent. For example, searching for "plumber Leicester" will often mean that someone needs a Leicester based plumber, and doesn't have a particular company in mind already.

We need to put ourselves in the shoes of the buyer. What are they likely to type into Google in order to buy your products or services? It's important to "enter the conversation in your prospect's mind". By understanding their thoughts, needs and desires, we can create an experience which they will immediately resonate with.

Before setting anything up in Google Ads, it's important to do all of the work required to develop your message. The benefit of this is to ensure that you understand your customers and more importantly their buying motives.

Potential Customer Personas

- **Browser** - The browser is looking for general information, they may be researching to buy, or they may be researching for a project they are working on. Some may go on to be interested; however many will never buy.
- **Shopper** - Interested in the product, but still researching, comparing products, checking reviews, comparing prices. Some could be ready to buy soon, some will take longer or not at all.
- **Buyer** - This is someone who is looking to buy right away. They know what they are looking for and require someone to sell it to them.

It's keywords which have a clear 'buying intent' coupled with being regularly searched (high search volume) that will often be the most profitable for your campaign.

Choosing Your Keywords

Choosing the right keywords can be the difference between success and failure in any campaign, so it's important to research thoroughly before getting started.

A simple way to commence your research is to follow these steps:

1. The place to start when conducting your keyword research is by getting the list of products and services we created in your message and using this as a starting point.
2. Take each product and list any synonyms or alternative names for these services. Try searching for them in Google to see what other companies are using.
3. Make a list of each of the areas you wish to cover in your campaign; this can include, cities, towns and possibly even counties.
4. Combine each of the variations of your keywords with each area you've identified. For example, you may have combined your keywords (boiler repair, boiler servicing and boiler installation) with your two main areas (Leicester and Nottingham) to generate
    boiler repair Leicester
    boiler servicing Leicester
    boiler installation Leicester
    boiler repair Nottingham
    boiler servicing Nottingham
    boiler installation Nottingham
5. Now you have your basic keyword list you'll want to get an idea of how many people are searching for these keywords on a monthly basis. Google Ads users will be able to find full search volumes by using the keyword section of Google Keyword Planner.
6. Order all of your data by monthly search volume and export this for use in a spreadsheet.
7. For the final stage, work out the top 20% of keywords based on search volume and add them into a free keyword tool like keywordtool.io. This step will

automatically provide you with a whole host of closely related keyword ideas based on Google's related searches feature.

8. Reimport the new list of keywords into Google Keyword Planner and export the data with final search volumes. Be sure to discard any keywords which don't have any monthly search volume and instead choose to focus on your best 'buying intent' options.

9. Repeat this process for each of your products and services.

Keyword Match Types:

When adding your final keywords into Google Ads, there are a number of different operators we can use to allow Google Ads to interpret the meaning of the keywords and give greater control over when ads should and shouldn't be shown.

Web Design Leicester	Broad match
"Web Design Leicester"	Phrase match
[Web Design Leicester]	Exact match
+Web +Design +Leicester	Broad match modifier

Web Design Leicester = Broad Match

Broad match will aim to show the advert whenever a user types in a combination of the words listed or any phrases which Google deems to be similar. This is a very risky way to add keywords as they can often result in showing your adverts to a larger number of searches, which will increase your spend but decrease your control.

E.g. Our advert could potentially be shown if someone types in "Web Design Leicester", "Website Designer Leicester", "Digital Agency in Leicester".

"Web Design Leicester" = Phrase Match

Phrase match works in a similar fashion to adding speech marks into a search term in Google. It will ensure that keywords are grouped and are required to appear only in your mentioned order. Phrase match is much better at closely targeting your keywords which are to be paid for.

E.g. Our advert will potentially be shown if someone types in "Web Design Leicester", "Best Web Design Leicester", "Web Design Leicester Reviews".

[Web Design Leicester] = Exact Match

Exact match does exactly what it describes, well kind of. It will only aim to show your advert if the user types in the keywords exactly as you have specified. It's worth noting that it will also include 'stop words' and operators such as *'in, from, to, of'* etc. This match type gives you the tightest amount of control over keyword use and should be used more prominently as the campaign begins to evolve. It might be tempting to set up the campaign using these, however *only* using exact match keywords will mean that many opportunities will be missed.
E.g. Our advert will potentially be shown if someone types in "Web Design Leicester", "Web Design in Leicester".

+Web +Design +Leicester = Broad Match Modifier
Broad match modifier is a very useful variation as it gives an added layer of flexibility whilst still keeping control. Every word which features '+' before it will be required to be present, but in any order. This match type is great to be used early on when initially setting up campaigns as it will generate a list of search terms which are being used and will provide a good starting point for further optimisation.
E.g. Our advert will potentially be shown if someone types in "Best Web Design companies in Leicester".

Negative keywords

So far we've only looked at keywords for which we would like our ads to show. However, a very powerful part of the process is the ability to state keywords for which we definitely *don't* want our ads to be shown. These keywords are called negative keywords and can be added at any stage to either ad group, campaign or account level.

An important part of the Google Ads optimisation process is monitoring 'search terms' for keywords that have generated clicks, but you would want to exclude in future. These can then be added as negative keywords to each campaign or to the whole account.

Key Metrics
Understanding the essential areas of your data is critical for interpreting the performance of the campaign and making incremental improvements.

- **Impressions** - This is the number of times your advert has been displayed to searchers.
- **Clicks** - The number of times your advert has been clicked.
- **Click through rate (CTR)** - The percentage of people that clicked from those who saw the impression.
- **Conversions** - The number of times people have gone on to complete a goal, such as complete a web form or make a phone call.
- **Conversion rate** - The percentage of people that converted from those that clicked.
- **Cost per conversion** - The average cost required for each conversion.
- **Cost per acquisition** - The average cost required for each paying customer (this cannot be tracked in Google Ads and will require you or your team to track your sales conversion offline).

Quality Score

Quality score is intended to give you a general sense of the quality of your ads. Each keyword in your campaign is given a score from 1-10 as an estimate of the quality of your ads and the landing pages they are directed to. Three factors determine your quality score:

- **Expected click-through rate**
- **Ad relevance** - how closely the copy in the advert matches the keyword
- **Landing page experience** - A number of factors including the average time spent on your page, the quality and relevance of your content, and how quickly your page loads.

Having a higher quality score means that Google thinks your ad and landing page are relevant and useful to someone looking at your ad. The higher the quality score, the lower each click could potentially cost.

Pricing, Bidding & Budgets

Google Ads is a platform built on a pay-per-click model. This means you will only be charged when someone clicks on your advert. If your main goal is to get people to visit your website, then clicks are a good place to start. Google Ads does offer pricing models based on impressions rather than clicks, but this is not something we would recommend using if you are focused on profit instead of brand awareness.

Google Ads is essentially an auction for which you can bid a given price for your desired keywords. Although positions aren't ordered based on price alone (they also consider quality and relevance), it will have a considerable impact on the overall ranking of your advert. Although your keyword pricing can initially be an estimate, you should ultimately aim to establish the maximum cost per click that you can afford to pay to acquire a new customer. Keyword prices can be set automatically by Google if you choose, however more advanced users like to keep close control of this aspect of the platform.

When configuring your campaign, it will be sensible to set budgets to limit the total amount Google will spend on your behalf. This limit will act as a safety net so that any silly mistakes don't result in financial catastrophe. Your budget in Google Ads can be specified at the campaign level and should denote the maximum amount you would be happy to spend each day. If you prefer to work out your budget on a monthly basis, simply divide your total monthly budget proportionately across your campaigns and then divide by 30.4 to reach a daily budget figure for each campaign.

As soon as your daily budget has been reached, your ads will cease to show until the following day. A question we get asked regularly is "how much should I spend?". The short answer is *as much as you can afford*. There is no right or wrong answer, and it will ultimately depend on the cash flow situation of your business and your desire to attract new leads.

If you are just starting out, I would advise taking things slowly at first to familiarise yourself with the platform and build your confidence. Once you start to get some initial results, you can begin to put your foot on the gas.

Advert Copywriting

Once we have the most effective keywords in place, crafting adverts which are both eye-catching and compelling to the target reader will ensure that your ad has the best chance of getting clicked over your competitors.

Website Design Leicester | Award-Winning Results - 100% Guaranteed
[Ad] www.gowebsites.co.uk/Website/Design ▾
★★★★★ Rating for gowebsites.co.uk: 4.7 - 108 reviews
At Least Double Your Local Leads In 90 Days or Your Full Money Back. Fast Turnaround, Award-Winning UK Team, Proven Results.
100% Increase In Leads · 90-Day Money-Back Guarantee · Fast Results · Great Reviews

FREE Marketing Toolkit   Reviews & Testimonials
Claim your free 10-step system for a   Learn how our customers businesses
consistent flow of new sales leads   have changed since using Go Websites

---

Example search advert including a rating, site links and call out extensions

Writing ads isn't an easy job, however, over time and with ongoing testing, it's possible for non-expert writers to create high performing campaigns. Here are a few tips for getting started.

- **Make the ad relevant to the keyword used** - Try to use the keyword exactly as it appears in the user's search term as this is what they will resonate with most. In our experience placing the keyword in the first heading usually has the most impact, therefore is a great place to start.
- **Speak in your customer's language** - You're not looking to win fancy writing awards for great style or wit, it's more about speaking in a clear language that your target customer understands and is familiar with.
- **Concise beats complex** - Try and maximise the impact from the space you have available with concise, fast flowing descriptions. Avoid using long wordy sentences.

- **Benefits first, features second** - Remember, the feature is what your product has or is going to do, the benefit is the emotional payoff they get for using your products.
- **Don't go over the top!** - Ensure your ads are not too hyped up as people tend to be sceptical. Try to be intriguing, but not pushy.
- **Use social proof** - State evidence that your product works where possible. This could include the number of reviews you've received, awards, accolades you've won, number of customers etc.
- **Use a compelling call to action** - Use words which create a sense of urgency and give clear instruction, e.g. "Buy Now And Save", "Download Now For Free".
- **Do a spelling and grammar check on your adverts** - This may seem simple, but it's easy to overlook. Bad spelling and grammar will give off a sloppy first impression.

Ad Extensions

When writing your advert copy, you'll also be able to benefit from the use of Google Ads extensions. Ad extensions are optional extras which can be added to your standard adverts in order to give them more detail or additional functionality. We would strongly recommend adding extensions as they are a great way to either create longer ads with more space for copy or simply take up more space on the page pushing your competitors' ads further down.

Here are a few of the most popular extension types at the time of writing this book. Google changes these regularly and often releases new extensions for testing. We would recommend strategically and systematically adding your extensions in order to monitor how they affect your existing performance.

Site Links

Site links are additional links which appear underneath your advert (sometimes with additional descriptions if your position permits this). This can be an excellent way to direct people quickly through to key pages on your website. For example, you could link to specific services, testimonials, pricing information or contact pages.

Site links are also a great way to ensure your advert takes up more space, pushing your competitors' ads further down the page.

Site links are shown at Google's discretion with a maximum of 4 appearing at any one time.

Callouts

Callouts are similar to site links but are not clickable. This makes them great for increasing the description length of your adverts. They will appear in a horizontal list format and can be a great way to share key benefits or unique selling points.

As with site links, they will be shown at Google's discretion with a maximum of 4 appearing at any one time.

Seller Rating Extension

When it comes to strengthening your marketing message, reviews from other people are one of the most effective methods to convince potential customers that you're the best choice to buy from. Remember, what others say about you is considerably more believable than what you say about yourself.

This extension is a fantastic way to show off your reputation, as it will allow you to display the little star icons as part of your advert. Getting your ratings to appear on your ads requires a regular stream of reviews and a current total of at least 150 or more within the last 12 months, and an overall score of 3.5 stars or above.

These reviews also have to have been submitted with one of around 35 approved Google approved suppliers like TrustPilot or Reviews.co.uk. If you're not currently in a position to use this, get to work on collecting reviews as this is one of the most powerful extensions in terms of increasing click-through rate.

Click To Call (Mobile Only)

Rather than clicking on your advert, users can click directly on a button which will in-turn start a phone call to your business. This minimises friction between seeing your adverts and speaking to your sales team.

Don't worry if you only have limited access to the phone, for example, 9am-5pm. It's easy to schedule the call extension to only show during business hours.

Location Extension

The Google Ads location extension is perfect for businesses looking to attract local customers to their premises. It allows businesses to display convenient details of where they are based and opening hours within the advert itself.

This ad extension is proven to increase the speed at which customers identify your location and contact details when planning a trip to your business. Many businesses advertise in areas where they are not based, so this extension can also help to validate your business location.

Message Extension

Rather than clicking on your advert or calling you directly, this smartphone targeted extension allows your prospect to send a message straight to your company using their messaging app.

When someone clicks on your ad, their message app will open and automatically become populated with a predefined message. This is very useful for attracting people who prefer to text rather than email or phone.

As with the click to call extension, the message extension can also be configured to show only during business hours.

Price Extension

When it comes to making a buying decision, price will always be a consideration for your customer. Some people are looking for the lowest prices, whilst others will see pricing as a gauge of quality and trust.

Prices can be displayed in many forms including, actual prices, hourly rates, prices from, prices up to and even zero pricing for promotional items or free trials. This may or may not work for your business, but it's a great way to increase the visibility of your adverts.

Structured Snippet Extension

Getting your message across effectively in such a small number of characters can be challenging. Use this extension to include an extra line of information about your products and services known as structured snippets.

This extension allows you to list additional data about your products or services from a number of predefined categories. This could include your services, brands, models, types, courses, amenities and several more.

Promotion Extension

Everybody loves to think they are getting a good deal; it's the logical side of our brain's way of justifying a purchase.

Google's promotion extension allows advertisers to display a special offer as a new line in your advert. Promotions can display discounted prices and even coupon codes which can be quoted when getting in touch.

Even if your business model doesn't lend itself to discounting, there are a number of clever ways in which you may still be able to benefit from this powerful tactic, and potentially make improvements to your overall campaign performance.

Testing & Optimisation

Surprisingly, the magic component which most Google Ads managers neglect is the very component which would allow them to continue to improve their ad performance - a solid testing programme.

Testing (or AB testing) is the process of creating a duplicate of the advert and slightly amending elements such as the headline copy. Google Ads will then run these two ads simultaneously for a short period of time until it is possible to decide on a winner.

We'll cover how to get started with testing in step 10 of the system, but until then, here are some tips for getting the most out of managing your campaign and ultimately the best return on your Google Ads investment.

- **Commit to regularly checking your account** - This might seem simple, but regularly logging into your account and actually performing a structured optimisation process could be one of the most valuable tasks you can undertake in your business. Not doing this is often the difference between getting this generating profit, and giving it up as a bad job.
- **Test your adverts** - When your adverts are running, you have two opportunities. The first is to be generating leads into your business. The second (and often overlooked) is the ability to test your marketing message, the copywriting and ad extensions with real-life customers. You should always have at least two ads running all of the time. If you only ever promote your winning ad, then your adverts will never stop improving.
- **Test your landing pages** - Exactly the same can be said with testing your website landing pages. Whilst you are driving traffic, there is a fantastic opportunity to improve the conversion rate of your key website pages.
- **In fact... test everything** - Once you start seeing the tangible benefits of your testing, you'll start to feel like you have a secret power over the rest of the non-testers out there, and you'll want to carry this into all aspects of your Google Ads campaign and more. Things you can test in Google Ads could include new keywords, pricing, locations, device types and much more.
- **Breakout your best performing keywords** - As soon as you know that a

keyword is performing well, be sure to break it out into a separate campaign and ad group. This way you can closely control the ads which are shown for this keyword as well as controlling the budget to ensure the lion's share of your spend is going on your most profitable keywords.

- **Regularly add negative keywords** - Negative keywords are a great way to keep your account in shape and keep wastage down to a bare minimum. Through each reporting period, you can generate a list of search terms which have resulted in clicks. Be sure to add any irrelevant terms to your campaigns to avoid them wasting click budget in the future.

CHAPTER 10

Traffic
Step 4. SEO

Have you ever been searching Google, only to wonder what causes some businesses to appear on the first page and others not? Google and other search engines have invested many years and huge amounts of money into figuring out how to best order each of the results.

As you would imagine, Search Engine Optimisation (SEO) is one of the most important and profitable components of your Local Marketing System. It has the power to bring you 'ready to buy' customers that are looking for the services you offer even if they've never heard of your company before.

The order in which Google decides to display results will have a huge impact on which business receives the most visitors and more importantly new leads.

If you've ever tried doing SEO yourself, or perhaps even hired an agency in the past to work on your behalf, you'll be no stranger to the amount of conflicting advice and technical jargon plastered around the web.

The sheer volume of information alone can often make getting started a difficult process, with many becoming paralysed from taking any action at all.

Getting consistent and stable rankings in Google requires experience and hard work to ensure that your website steadily climbs up in the results positions and stays there for years to come.

As with all aspects of our local marketing system, we've been able to develop our processes based on years of getting great results in real businesses spanning across lots of industries. It's this experience which we're going to be sharing with you throughout this chapter.

What is SEO?

Let's start with some of the basics. SEO or Search Engine Optimisation is the process of managing your website's technical structure, content and reputation on the web in order to build credibility, which in turn moves your page higher up the organic search rankings.

Types Of Search Results

When you type a keyword or key phrase into Google to look for a service in your local area, you'll get a page of results broken down into the following recognisable types and positions.

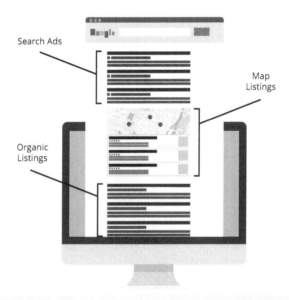

Diagram of listing types which may appear on a typical search results page

a) Search Ads

These are the paid Google Ads listings which we covered in the last chapter.

b) Map Listings

Map listings are results which are displayed based on the user's current location, or the area which they've included in their search term. An example of this would be for the term 'wedding catering London'. These are naturally ranked and therefore will benefit from the work you are doing in this chapter.

c) Organic Listings

Organic is the word for the 'natural' listings which appear further down the page and are ordered purely on reputation and relevance alone. It's quite common for some Google users to scroll down past the adverts and map listings to these more 'trusted' results.

Nobody is paying Google directly to be featured here, and there are many other factors which Google uses to decide on the ordering.

It's these organic rankings that should be prioritised as part of your ongoing SEO campaign.

Benefits Of SEO

- **Ready to buy traffic** - Out of all the marketing which your business can undertake, nothing is more effective than getting yourself in front of people who are actively searching for your products and services at that very moment in time. These people are most likely to need your services right away making them fully qualified and the easiest to convert into paying customers.
- **Positioning and credibility** - When your business appears in the most prominent positions, you'll start to be looked upon as the leader in your field by both potential customers and competitors alike. This kind of positioning

will help to build trust and gain authority in your field.

- **Around the clock sales leads** - Organic search engine rankings achieved by SEO will be consistently visible 24 hours a day. Unlike paid ads, they won't stop appearing when your budget runs out.
- **Most trusted results in Google** - Organic results from SEO are still the most trusted results of all types (including ads which sit at the very top). Approximately 65-75% of users will skip past the ads in favour of these more 'credible' rankings, citing lack of trust in the ads as the most popular reason.
- **Fully trackable return on investment** - As with all digital marketing efforts, SEO can be fully quantified, allowing you to trace your spend to the nearest penny and attribute which parts of your marketing system are working most efficiently.

Getting Started With SEO

Here's a diagram of a basic organic listing on a typical search engine results page (SERP).

Go Websites: The No.1 Award-Winning Local Marketing System
https://www.gowebsites.co.uk/ ▼
At least double your local leads in 90 days or less 100% guaranteed. Order your copy of 'The Ultimate Local Marketing Toolkit' for FREE. Take your first step towards a more profitable business today...

An example of an organic listing including the clickable page title (max 60 characters), the destination web address (max 75 characters) and the page description (max 300 characters) provided by your meta description.

Choosing Your Keywords

Choosing your keywords for SEO is a straightforward process. Having already done your keyword research as part of your Google Ads setup, choosing your keywords simply requires you to check your Google Ads for your best performing buyer intent keywords.

This means you can reduce the risk of investing all of this time only to find out the keywords you are optimising don't convert. If you don't have enough Google Ads data, focus on this first.

Keyword Distribution

Now you have your keywords identified, you will need to find the best places to include them on your website. It's important to ensure that each keyword (or very closely related groups of keywords) is optimised on its own page ensuring Google is clear on the subject matter of this page.

Failure to do this can result in confusion over which page is to be ranked, and may result in both pages becoming less effective.

Getting Started With SEO

Now that you have your keywords in place, here's a short explanation as to how to approach your SEO strategy and get the best results for driving in new traffic. Remember SEO is not a quick process and will take consistent and continued effort, but the results will be worth the wait.

The benefit of having your pages display in organic results is that it doesn't cost you per click, meaning that your ROI can often be much higher and your listing is visible 24 hours a day. On the flip side, organic rankings for competitive keywords can take a lot of time and effort to achieve, and the unpredictability and fluctuation of the search results can be frustrating.

Google has developed an extremely intricate system to rank individual pages known as its algorithm. This equation takes into consideration many factors, including the quality, relevance and originality of the content, through to the number of pages linking back to you from the rest of the internet. It's estimated that there are over 1000 individual flags which have varying degrees of weighting to how they influence ranking.

There are three fundamental aspects of SEO which you will need to consider when optimising your website for the best search engine performance.

Technical

The first place to start with SEO is the technical aspect. As a business owner or marketing manager you might not have the technical experience to work on these aspects yourself, but don't panic, it is not important for you to be able to complete this work yourself, more so that you are able to instruct your developer on getting these components in place to a satisfactory level. Some of the items described below may require changes to be made to your website from a developer with experience in technical SEO.

Good Quality Coding

Having a carefully constructed and well-coded website is the foundation of technical SEO. Ensuring that your page uses the most appropriate HTML tags (including heading tags) in the correct order will help search engines to understand what you deem to be the most important content on the page. Things like broken images or missing files can cause delays when loading and in turn, seriously slow down your website and negatively impact your user's experience and SEO.

Page Speed

Given the recent swing to mobile web, page speed has never been more important. Whilst internet connections may be fast whilst you're browsing at home, many users are still connecting via 3G connections or lower whilst they are on the go. Ensuring your website loads fast will not only help your SEO performance, it will also improve your chances of conversion. The best way to analyse your website speed on a technical level is using Google's PageSpeed Insights, which can be found at https://developers.google.com/speed/pagespeed/insights/. This quick test will provide you with a score out of 100 for both mobile and desktop versions of your website, whilst giving your developer a full breakdown of how to improve this score.

Structured data

Structured data has been around for a while now, and is basically a way of adding context to particular types of data. For example, if your business collects customer reviews and they are listed on your website, rather than just being written as plain content, you can structure a review in a certain format (also called a schema) to let search engines know this is a review. For example, according to the schema, a review should have a title, an author, a description, a maximum score, a lowest score and the score which the author awarded the service they received.

The benefit of using structured data like this is that Google may choose to show your review in the form of stars underneath the headline for your business's listing on the search results page.

Taylor Pickering: Plumbers Leicester & Electricians Leicester
★★★★★ Rating: 4.6 - 25 Reviews
https://www.taylorpickering.com/ ▼
Taylor Pickering is an award-winning electrical and plumbing service provider. Guaranteed workmanship from a company you can trust.

Example of how your listing could appear in Google's search results page with review schema enabled in your code.

There are many different types of schema which can be utilised to your advantage when it comes to SEO. A full list of these can be found at Schema.org.

SSL Certificate

An SSL certificate is a service which is added by your web hosting provider and securely encrypts data as it travels from your website through to your user's device or computer. Without an SSL certificate in place, your website data can technically be intercepted at any point it passes through along the way.

Not only is this a sensible thing to have in place for general data protection and the new GDPR law, but it's also now considered a 'flag' for ranking websites. Websites without an SSL certificate could be negatively impacted in the search results according to Google.

The way to tell if a website is using an SSL is to look carefully at the website address. SSL secured websites will start with https:// instead of http://

Google Search Console

As the owner of a website which is responsible for generating a ready supply of leads, you'll soon realise the importance of ensuring it remains in good health. Search Console is a free service provided by Google which helps to keep an eye on problems relating to your website. This could include broken links, broken page redirects or sudden changes in your website's situation. Ensure this is set up by your web designer and that they are receiving notifications in case they occur.

Wordpress Plugins & Tools

If your website is built using Wordpress, there are a number of plugins which you might want to ensure are installed to help with your SEO campaign.

- **Yoast SEO** - This is the industry standard plugin for keeping track of the SEO on your website. Not only will it help to fix a number of default issues with Wordpress itself, but it also comes with a real-time scoring system for how well your page content has been optimised.
- **301 Redirects** - This plugin will help you to correctly redirect pages that are no longer relevant to avoid '404 page not found' errors for your visitors.
- **W3Total Cache** - Cache or caching (pronounced 'cash' or 'cashing') is the process of compiling your website's code so that it can be quickly accessed without needing to read the database. The important end-result of this is that your Wordpress website can be made to run much faster.

Content Optimisation

Getting the quality of your content right is arguably the most important individual ranking factor, and this alone could have a huge impact not only on your rankings but also on your conversion rate. You may have heard the SEO phrase 'content is king' well, my advice is to treat it like royalty.

Look at your content as an opportunity to excel. Provide the customer with every single bit of information they need to make a decision and more. This will not only increase your chances of getting better search engine results, if done properly, it could also increase the rate at which these pages convert traffic into paying customers.

Put yourself in Google's shoes for a moment. A user has just entered a search for "landscape gardener Manchester", it's deciding which order to show competing pages in the organic listings. It's going to look for overall credibility, but let's for a moment assume that all other factors are equal and it comes down to the quality and originally of the content.

When search engine's read your content, they do so with the aim of establishing what your content is about and how useful it will be to the searcher. Google's sophistication in this area is somewhat greater than it used to be in years gone by.

Whereas it used to be recommended to place your desired keywords in as many places as possible on your page, this is no longer the case.

The best advice from an SEO standpoint is to focus on making original content that is useful for your reader. This means writing for humans, not for search engines. It's important to include keywords (which we'll cover shortly) but only have them in a way which naturally suits the flow of your writing.

Here are some of the key page elements that will require some careful consideration when creating pages in order to drive organic traffic.

Page Title & Descriptions

The page title is the name of the page and is visible in the browser tab at the very top of the browser window. Further to this, it is visible whenever the page is shared through another platform like on Facebook or Twitter. Just like the title of a newspaper article, the title is paramount and therefore should contain your keywords.

Heading Tags

Heading tags (denoted using <h1> to <h6>) are clear ways to both break up your content and to inform the user about what your page or sections of your page are likely to be talking about. These are again, an excellent opportunity to naturally include your keywords or related words, and have a high weight of importance for SEO.

Body Content

Body content is the word for all of the text which is included in your article on your page. The most important thing for your body content is that your copywriting is original and not copied from any other websites such as your suppliers or competitors. In terms of how long your pages should be, we would recommend 500 words or more, however, spend more time thinking about how it can be of value to your customer rather than simply aiming for an exact word count.

Internal Links

Links in your content which point to other optimised pages on your site are known as internal links. Even though they are situated on your website, they are still able to add value by passing SEO strength known as 'link juice'. Internal links are great for adding value to your key pages but only when an opportunity appears naturally, and when it will be of benefit to the reader. Too many links on your page will dilute the effectiveness from an SEO perspective so keep this to a maximum of 3-4 per page if possible.

Images

Images on your optimised pages will help in many aspects of your marketing. Using good quality images which are relevant to your topic will help to hold your reader's interest and also appeal to the more visually responsive user. From an SEO perspective, the way that images are formatted will help search engines to understand what the graphic is depicting. Use images that are in line with the subject of your content and your keywords, and be sure to include a clear 'Alt' (Alternative text) tag and name your files in a meaningful manner. An example of this would be to name the file landscape-gardener-working-in-southampton.jpg rather than DCS0672.jpg.

Page URLs

A page URL or as they are called in Wordpress, slug or permalink, is the address which someone will use to reach your page. As with other aspects of your page, make sure your URL helps to clearly describe the topic of your page. It will also be beneficial to include keywords in the URL where possible and keep the total length (including the main domain part) down to a size of 60 characters or less.

Link Building

Getting other websites to link back to yours will increase its credibility and show that your website must be valuable as other pages are putting their reputation on the line by vouching for it.

Back in the old days of SEO, Google mainly considered quantity over quality, meaning that links from literally anywhere would accumulate to build strength.

However, we're long past those days now. Google carefully analyses the inter-relationship of pages linking to other pages and decides which ones are most trustworthy.

Imagine I've got a friend called Tony, and he likes his wine. Well that's an understatement, he loves his wine, and he certainly does know his Claret from his Beaujolais. His passion for wine is borderline obsessive. If I needed a recommendation for a particular meal or occasion, then I'd wait with baited breath on his response and trust what Tony says implicitly, because he's the biggest authority I know on the subject.

Now two months down the line, I find I need some rewiring doing in my house. I'm not thinking about Tony at this point, because as far as I'm aware, he knows absolutely nothing about electrics. I'd feel much safer calling a qualified electrician.

Google looks at links in a similar way. If the link comes from an authoritative and credible source which is related to the topic of your page, then it's given more weight than if it comes from an unknown and unrelated site.

Think of links from two perspectives. An opportunity to build the authority of your page and an opportunity to drive related traffic to your page. If the traffic opportunity is poor, then the authority value of the link is likely to be less.

Building links to a website is not an easy game and will require some extremely creative thinking at times, but here are a few techniques to get you started.

1. Guest Blogging

Blogging is an excellent way to both drive traffic and position yourself as an expert.

This is certainly the case when your article is published as a special feature by someone else. There are many blog owners out there who have built up fantastic followings through their commitment to publishing regular content. Their biggest problem is that quality content takes time to create. For this reason, there are sites out there which will happily allow you to publish good quality content on their blog in exchange for a link back to your website.

The best way to approach this is to identify a list of blogs which would be both related to your industry and would benefit from having a guest blog post. Once you have this, conduct some simple due diligence and see what content would work for their site. This helps to demonstrate that you've already invested effort and are serious about this, not just asking anyone and everyone.

You could even write the content plan ahead of time to reduce their need to imagine possible subject matter.

2. Infographic

Evidence shows, one of the most shareable pieces of content a business can create is useful information presented in an exciting visual format. This could take the form of diagrams, charts, graphs, tables and more. Collectively they are known as Infographics.

Think about how key information relating to your industry could be represented visually, and how it could appeal to your target audience. The better your resource, the more likely other people will be prepared to link to it from their own websites too.

Once you have completed your infographic, there are also a number of infographic distribution websites which will help to promote it to a wider audience including sharing it using social media.

3. Influencer Outreach

There are many websites, blogs or authorities which have developed a fantastic reputation in the eyes of their readers and indeed with search engines. Why not reach out to several influential resources with the ultimate aim of requesting a link to a helpful article on your website, which their readers may find useful.

The best way to have success with this approach is to ask them to link to something of greater value. If you have a guide, blog post, video or even infographic which will be of interest to their readers, then it's infinitely more likely that they'll consider taking you up on your offer.

Getting success with this method is difficult and will require persistence, but the links which are generated are often extremely valuable in helping your SEO campaign.

4. Digital Press Release

Whereas news articles have traditionally been written by journalists for newspapers and magazines, the number one host of news content today is on the internet. A press release is a way of packaging your news announcements to be issued to news organisations and journalists.

Getting your information in front of people in the form of a digital press release is a great way to attract both good links and publicity at the same time. Why not plan to research, write and distribute your news with the aim of attracting links from other websites as well as potentially being featured in popular news sites such as Google News and many others.

5. Resources Page Links

Many websites list resources which they feel could be useful to their visitors or customers in the form of a links or resources page. Getting your website listed as a useful resource will not only help to build your SEO but can also drive visitors through to your site too.

6. Broken Link Finding

The internet is full of websites containing links to other pages. It's only natural that a given proportion of these links will either no longer exist or be broken. Identifying websites related to your industry which may feature broken link opportunities can be a great reason to get in touch.

By making the website owner aware of the issue with their site, you can build goodwill and hopefully create an opportunity to replace their broken link with an equally informative link to an article from your website.

7. Skyscraper Technique

As with many things in life, there is a significant advantage to be gained from finding something that is working currently and aiming to emulate and improve on its success. The skyscraper technique is where we identify a high performing piece of content that may already exist in your industry, which has evidence of it being regularly linked to and shared on social media.

The article could be a 'how to' guide, or a detailed breakdown of everything that needs to be considered by a buyer before they make a decision to commit and hire a company like yours.

Once you have found a suitable subject, aim to create a new piece of content which is even more useful. It could go deeper into the subject or just provide a more exhaustive account. This will give you a valuable asset which can be used as 'link bait' when reaching out with any of the techniques we've described so far.

8. Content Commenting

A great way to interact with readers is through commenting. Comments can be added to videos on YouTube as well as the majority of blog posts or forums. Why not find and watch a useful video which relates to your product or service and then post an engaging and positive comment. In the comment, you could leave a natural link to your website and even share the video via your social media channels to build more rapport.

Although these links are often not as valuable from an SEO perspective, they can be a great way to drive meaningful traffic to your website.

9. Directories & Citations

Last but not least in terms of link building, a great way to build links is to identify business directories that appear on the web. There are literally thousands of websites which are designed for bringing together like-minded businesses in the hope of creating a useful resource.

Many directories will allow you to write a short profile and share details about your business, products or services, opening hours, prices, payment methods and of course a link to your website.

Even if the directory doesn't allow you to create an actual link to your website, it can be a great way to show Google that you have a genuine business at the address provided. These are known as citations and are also proven to help your long term SEO campaign.

CHAPTER 11

Traffic
Step 5. Social Media

Social media and the ease of its accessibility is single-handedly the biggest social change in the world this millennium. So much so, that it's almost difficult to remember what life was actually like before it existed.

Whether you are actively using Facebook, Twitter, Instagram, etc. on a personal level or whether you've purposefully steered away from it, there's no hiding the fact that it's here to stay and that your business has a wonderful opportunity to prosper from it.

For many years, advertising has been a one-way conversation, but now the game has changed! It's time to ensure that your business is moving with the times and is protected long into the future.

For most businesses, getting started on social media consists of setting up a profile in your business' name and starting to post and engage with other people. Whilst the first few days or even weeks can feel like fun, it quickly becomes apparent that inspiration and commitment often starts to drop off.

Even if your willpower to keep committed to social media is strong, you eventually start to look at the effectiveness of your posting and how much return you are getting in terms of sales. Social media is such a huge opportunity, why is it that so many businesses have yet to find a way to monetise their efforts and ultimately turn a profit from their investment?

They often focus on the detail and not on the bigger strategy. Social media is exactly what its name suggests, a media channel. Just like telephone, email and SMS are all forms of media too.

It's a vehicle for sharing your message, not the message itself. You wouldn't simply email someone every day simply because you have their email address, or call them every day because you have their phone number?

Although social media is different in some ways, fundamentally, your success depends on how meaningful your message is, and how well it aligns with your customers' desires, dreams, hopes and fears.

We've cut our teeth in social media through posting and analysing the success of tens of thousands of real-life posts. During this time, we've been able to discover what works and what doesn't work when it comes to creating interesting, engaging and ultimately profitable content.

What Is Social Media?

To keep things simple, social media is the collective name for the use of social networking. Social networks are websites or apps where people can go to interact or 'network' with others. Each network may often have its own unique features or target demographic, but fundamentally all social networks allow users to:

- Create profiles for themselves or their business.
- Allow you to publish content to these profiles. E.g. messages, photos, videos etc.
- Engage with other people's profiles to build a network. E.g. sharing, liking, commenting etc.

Most social networks are free to their users, with revenue streams being generated from advertising as the platform grows in popularity and usage.

Types Of Social Media Posting

When it comes to posting on social networks, there are usually two ways of doing so, each with their own benefits.

A: Organic Posting

Organic social media posting is when you use the platform as it was intended for its core users. This means you've created a profile and are regularly posting content in the form of messages, images, videos, links to your website etc. Organic posting is free, and it is great for sharing content amongst the people that you already have in your network, for example, they are following you or have liked your page.

B: Adverts

Most of the bigger networks have developed advertising platforms which can be used by business customers in order to buy views of their content from people who are not in their immediate network. In particular, with Facebook and Twitter, advertisers can build an 'audience' to whom they can show their adverts. Your audience can be targeted based on demographics, age, interests, financial status and much more. Although adverts are very much a part of social media, we'll discuss them in more detail in the Facebook ads section of your local marketing system which is coming later in the book.

Choosing Your Platforms

With the list of potential platforms growing by the day, it's easy to become overwhelmed with which platforms to invest your precious time and hard-earned money into. Although there are undoubtedly potential benefits for being an early adopter of new networks, we would almost certainly recommend sticking with the platforms which already have the largest user bases, and match your ideal customer profile.

Here is a selection of the most popular platforms you may consider.

Facebook

Facebook is by far the biggest of the social platforms and has the largest number of active users. For this reason, we would recommend that most businesses choose this as the primary network to share their content. Facebook is generally more popular with adults and also with older generations. Even grandparents are now starting to use Facebook where they haven't in the past.

Twitter

Twitter is one of the most commonly quoted and publicised platforms, especially by other traditional news sources. With so many of the world's authorities on sports, politics and entertainment using Twitter, users often spend much longer browsing the platform.

Instagram & Snapchat

Instagram and Snapchat may be suitable if your target market is a younger generation. In terms of active user base, Instagram is actually a larger network than Twitter, and both Instagram and Snapchat are regarded as 'fashionable' platforms which your children are most likely to be using.

LinkedIn

If your target customers are primarily businesses, then LinkedIn is a great opportunity to network and build your profile with content. Many people maintain their LinkedIn profile as an extension of their CV making it a great place to discover individual people within organisations. Whilst many users will also be using the likes of Facebook, many will ensure that their engagement in LinkedIn is in line with the professional reputation they wish to convey.

Benefits Of Social Media

- **Social proof** - Social media is a great way to demonstrate that people are interacting with your messages, company and products and in turn demonstrating that you are trustworthy and worth paying attention to.
- **Millions of potential customers** - With over half of the UK's population active on Facebook on a daily basis, there really is no other single place where your customers are congregating online on this scale. This is a huge

opportunity that many businesses have yet to tap into.

- **Build authority and expertise** - It has never been easier to be seen as an expert, yet so few people are actually achieving this. With regular contributions over prolonged periods of time, you'll start to be viewed as passionate and committed to your trade or industry.
- **Demonstrate proactiveness** - When it comes to choosing businesses to work with, one of the most important factors cited is communication. How punctual is this business at getting back to its customers? Regular posting on social media is often an indicator people use to see how responsive your communication is likely to be.
- **Engage with your customers** - One of the most underrated truths about social media is that this platform is *two-way communication*. Not only can you broadcast out to your customers, but you also need to be listening in. Hearing your customers' problems and needs is a great way to connect on a personal level and build rapport.

Uses For Social Media in Business

Here is a small list of things that social media can be used for:

- Spreading positive messages about your company
- Keeping in contact with your existing customers
- Educating and inspiring your followers
- Reaching new potential customers
- Handling public relations (PR) issues
- Promoting offers and new products
- Running paid advertising campaigns

Getting Started With Social Media

There are so many ways to approach social media. It can be challenging to get started if you don't know which way to turn. As you're well aware by now, we like to employ an organised and systematic approach. Random creation of posts will ultimately become hard to manage and tiring, so before we start writing any content, I'd recommend getting your plan in shape.

Content Calendar

Social media is often about what's happening *today*. Things move quickly, and yesterday's news is soon forgotten. By developing a bespoke content calendar, you'll be able to plan ahead for events that happen throughout the year and make sure you never miss a trick.

A content calendar is a central document which can be easily put together in Word or Excel. This is your place to keep a note of important events that will be occurring throughout the year. Your events could be based on the seasons, themes, festivals and other well-known occasions which happen throughout the year in your business and in the wider world.

This will help to ensure that you can create content, promotions and relationships at key times of the year.

Here are a few ideas to get you started:

- Seasons and holidays
- Industry/trade show events
- Local events
- Sporting and entertainment events
- Milestones in your business
- Product launches
- Peak selling seasons

Posting Guidelines

Posting guidelines are essentially a set of rules which help you to keep your voice, tone and personality consistent whilst you're posting on behalf of your business. Whether it's the things you talk about, the style of images you use or even quirky words or phrases you're known for using when you communicate.

Your posting guidelines document should be made easily accessible to anybody who will be creating content on behalf of your company. Today this might be yourself, but tomorrow it could be one of your team or even an external agency.

Your posting guidelines should include things like:

- Writing style, personality and tone
- Distinctive words and phrases you use when you talk
- Things you should mention often
- Things you shouldn't mention at all
- Breakdown of post types that you cover (we'll cover more on post types shortly)
- Monthly post breakdown (30 days), see example below

Example breakdown of daily post ideas
6 x social validation posts (e.g. testimonials, reviews, case studies)
5 x events related posts
4 x product or services/sales related posts
4 x links to previous educational blog posts
4 x useful tips and advice posts
3 x promoting monthly offers posts
2 x staff social events and photos
1 x customer of the month post
1 x employee of the month posts

You'll always be able to ensure that you're working towards the same goals by sticking to an agreed blueprint for the types of posts you create and how frequently you publish them.

There may be times when rigidly sticking to this isn't possible, but by having a clear plan, you'll end up with a system for coming up with ideas, and know what to look for when seeking good content opportunities. Like with most things in business, forming positive habits will make the job easier in time.

Furthermore, as time passes, you'll be able to learn from the performance of previous posts to further improve and enhance your future posting guidelines.

Setting Up Your Social Media Profile Pages

Whichever platforms you decide to go with, you'll have the ability to personalise them inline with your brand and more importantly the marketing message you developed in step one of the system. Here are some of the most important things to consider when setting up your profile pages.

Choosing Your Usernames

If you don't already have a profile, then the first thing will be to register your usernames (also called handles). It's recommended to try and keep your usernames the same. This means that potential customers can both find and recognise your profile without any hassle. However, given the number of usernames which will have already been taken, and the character limits often imposed, it might not always be possible. Try and keep your names short and easily recognisable as your company.

Branding

Again, in the pursuit of simplicity and clarity for your prospects, it's critical to keep your branding completely consistent with your website or landing page. Use exactly the same logo, colours, photos and styles. This will make it extremely easy for your customers to know they are in the right place.

Your Message

If you haven't already, you'll soon realise that your message is one of the most important factors in connecting with your customers on an emotional level. Use this opportunity to reiterate your message, by including your USP, benefits and your offer in the most prominent places.

Image Types And Sizes

Each of the most popular social media platforms allow you to upload personalised images. These will vary depending on platform; however, they often change specification as they make ongoing improvements. Popular image types that you might find are:

- **Header image** - This will be a horizontal image which sits across the top of your profile.
- **Profile image** - This is often a square image which will be used as a thumbnail every time you make or interact with a post.
- **Background image** - Some may allow you to include a large background image which appears whilst people are viewing your profile.

Social Media Meta Tags

In recent years, you'll have noticed if you post a link on Facebook, Twitter or a number of other platforms, it often turns your link into a post which features an image, a headline and a description. This happens automatically and the information is taken from social media metadata. This could be an image which is already featured on your page, or it can be specified for each page by using a suitable Wordpress plugin like Yoast SEO. I would recommend configuring this yourself to control what is displayed when people share your link. Again, this is a great opportunity to use compelling copywriting.

Writing Your Content

For some people, this is the fun part, but for others, it feels more like an obstacle. Knowing what to write can be very difficult. In fact, doing anything creative without first having inspiration can be challenging. Inspiration can hit you at any moment, sometimes in the strangest of places, but if you don't want to have to wait for a momentary flash of creativity, then you can follow our proven structure for categorising and generating ideas for your social media.

We have eight main categories, which are broken down further into example items which could be used in order to create ideas. Whilst you're reading through this list, it's extremely handy to have a pen and paper to record the ideas as they come into your head.

1. Events

Events are very good for social media engagement as they are often already being promoted by the organiser and have a clear start and end date. This makes it easy to focus your efforts on piggybacking their marketing during this period. Here are some popular event types:

- **Company events** - Events which relate specifically to your business. These could include taster days, seminars, launch parties, new product releases, new booking windows being opened etc.
- **Business milestones dates** - Key dates that relate specifically to your business, such as when it started, milestone ages, anniversaries for important events, awards, accreditations or achievements.
- **Industry events** - Events or shows which relate more broadly to your industry, sector or customer-base. These could include conferences, exhibitions, important deadlines, initiatives etc.
- **Seasonal events and trends** - Events that are specifically related to a particular time of year. These could include Christmas, Easter, Diwali, Valentines etc. This is a perfect time to mention seasonal trends for product sales or customer requirements. E.g. Winter tyre sales start in October.
- **Local events** - Are there any events happening in your local area? They can be related specifically to your location rather than your industry. Mentioning or supporting local events can be a great way to build a sense of community and rapport with businesses and residents alike.
- **Sports and entertainment events** - Are there any significant sporting or entertainment events that are held in your local area which could be beneficial to support? Do you have an affinity with the club or event, or could it be used as a way to reach people in your target demographic?
- **Random days (Days of the year)** - Random days are a fun way to theme your posts. There are numerous themes happening every day, so it's quite easy to

find days that are related to your industry. These posts are generally more fun orientated so we would recommend using these sparingly. Examples of random days include Cheese Lovers Day, Employee Appreciation Day, National Tea Day and thousands more.

- **Awareness days** - Awareness days are similar to random days but from a more serious perspective of raising awareness and supporting good causes. You can be seen promoting important work and events, whilst increasing visibility of your business in the process. Examples of awareness days include Dry January, National Friendship Day, World Animal Day and many more.

2. Friends & Network

Social media is all about creating conversations. Identifying and mentioning specific people will notify the user, and increase the likelihood they'll like, share or reply to your post. People feel good when they are talked about or praised and are more likely to get involved in return.

- **Nearby businesses** - Are there any local businesses who you can reach out to? Businesses that you know personally are more likely to engage with our posts if you mention them. It will help to build a sense of community, especially with those that have an affinity with your business, services or products.
- **Suppliers** - Are there any key suppliers or service providers which your company currently uses and is publicly happy to mention? You could praise them for great service or commitment to your business over the years.
- **Friends and family** - Do you have any family members or friends who are particularly active on social media? Providing their posts and opinions are professionally aligned with your company values, they can be a great way to increase your exposure and engagement.
- **Customers** - Can you mention any of your valued customers, thanking them, promoting their products and services, upcoming events, praising their achievements, or retweeting their messages? Be sure to capture plenty of images when they drop by your business premises or attend events.
- **Staff and associates** - Can you mention staff members for their achievements or when they take part in notable events? This could be Birthdays, promotions, awards, training days, team building days, celebrations, working

on a key project, sharing a testimonial, or other positive occasions.

- **Thought leaders** - Are there any widely accepted experts in your field? They could be people who have an existing following or perhaps have been published for their work? They do not have to be particularly known to your customers in order to benefit from their potential reach or credibility.
- **Celebrities** - Can you mention or interact with celebrities if they talk about your industry or subject matter? They don't have to be talking about your business in particular, but you could gain valuable exposure if you were seen to be sharing expert opinions with well-known people.
- **Politicians and counsellors** - Can you mention politicians or council members who talk about or conduct work which is related to your business or subject matter? Again, they don't have to be talking about your business specifically to benefit from this.

3. Products And Services (For Sales)

Although many people will say that social media isn't about selling, it is important to ensure you are promoting your products and services. People who avoid selling will be foolishly leaving potential money on the table. Sales related posts should be kept to a maximum of 20% of your overall post total.

- **Features and key benefits** - Social media is a great place to talk about your products, services and specifically the benefits of using them. This is also a good opportunity to create links back to your key pages, offers or calls to action.
- **Product photos** - Make sure you have lots of photos, pictures or diagrams, especially if it helps to make the product easier to understand or to sell the benefits. See the photos section for more inspiration on how you can use photos to your advantage.
- **Unique selling proposition (USP)** - Explain the reasons why your business should be chosen over all other competitors and alternatives. Furthermore, you could also break them down into smaller 'unique selling points' to use and share in your posts.
- **Comparisons** - Can you make public comparisons to highlight the benefit of choosing your products or services over alternative ones? This should always

be done in a tasteful and non-confrontational manner, aiming to educate the reader about the benefits.

- **Problems solved** - Describe problems which your product or service helps to solve. These could range from little frustrations related to buying the product or larger problems that your product will help to fix or remove.

4. Useful Information (For Education)

One of the best directions for social media content is to share information that helps to educate people as to how they can resolve issues or be empowered to make good decisions when buying. These posts are more likely to be received well and even shared by others.

- **How-to videos** - Can you share videos with the aim of educating and demonstrating expertise in your field? If you don't have any yourself, you could always share from YouTube.
- **Free guides** - Can you share links to any free guides or content you have produced? Alternatively, you could use industry/government produced guides, research projects, supplier guides or even manufacturer guides if possible.
- **Handy websites/blogs** - Can you share links, articles or stories from industry related websites? These could include blog posts, forums, consumer awareness, educational, supplier, manufacturer or even government / local authority websites.
- **Tips and tricks** - Are there any useful nuggets of insight that you can provide to help or add value to your customers' lives? Often these tips may feel too simple or basic, but remember your customers don't have the technical knowledge which you possess.
- **Quotes** - Quotes can be an excellent conversation starter and can be related to your industry, funny, insightful, motivational, etc. They can also be linked back to key benefits, e.g. saving time, money, making life easier etc.
- **Industry statistic share** - Statistics can be very visual and easy to interpret at a glance. Can you use statistics that relate to customers, problems, or general trends in the industry?
- **Answer an FAQ** - As the expert, you will no doubt get asked many of the

same questions over and over. It doesn't matter how small and simple they seem to you, it's often this 'entry-level' insight which provides the most value to potential customers.

- **Share infographics** - Infographics are diagrams, charts or drawings which help to illustrate information. This could include industry statistics, industry trends, industry history, company history, company processes, benefits, results, achievements, etc.
- **Latest company news** - Can you share exciting company news such as introducing new employees, staff awards, accreditations, new partnerships, annual reviews, etc.
- **Recent blog post** - Your blog may contain useful content you can link to. This could include seasonal posts, key quotes from posts, or posing questions which are answered in the post.

5. Offers & Promotions

Use monthly promotions to attract attention and encourage people to take action. It's quite possible that you're already running promotions, but not utilising your social network to get them in front of more people. Promotions don't always just have to be about offering money off. Here are some additional ideas to get you started:

- **Promo codes** - Can you create dedicated promotional codes to be redeemed against offers including a *percentage discount (e.g. 20% off)*, *a flat rate amount discount (e.g. £20 off)*, *discount when you spend a certain amount, free bonus gift, free month* etc.
- **Referrals / recommend a friend** - Why not run a promotion to encourage your customers to refer their friends? Formats could include *refer a friend and receive a cash sum, receive a voucher/discount for a future purchase, receive a free gift (for referrer or both parties)*.
- **Twitter competition** - Competitions are an extremely popular way to get your network excited and grow your followers. Can you offer a prize in order to host a Twitter competition or giveaway? Users can enter by liking, retweeting or providing the best answers to a given question.
- **Flash sale** - A flash sale is a promotion that is offered for a very short period

of time or for only a small number of fast-acting people. Flash sale examples could include the *first person to reply, first five people to reply, anyone replies over the weekend*. Other angles could be to get their friends involved with flash sales such as *most deserving customer, most in need of a makeover*, or simply *nominate a friend*.

- **Photo contest** - People love to get their moment in the limelight. Challenge your users to submit photos of themselves inline with your guidelines. They could be using your products or enjoying the benefits of your finished work. Incentivise or reward their entry by offering to share their photos or provide a free gift for all entries/winners.

- **Free trials and samples** - Nothing sparks excitement and overcomes objections like a 'try before you buy' offer. Is it possible to offer a free sample, trial, taster session, appraisal, consultation, proposal or viewing in order to entice potential leads into your business?

6. Social Validation

Using social validation to demonstrate the popularity of your product or service will help to convince others that your business is trustworthy.

- **Customer testimonials** - Testimonials allow people to view your products and services through the eyes of someone with similar problems and concerns. You could include written testimonials from your website, full case studies featured as blogs, success stories, reviews on 3rd-party websites.

- **Video testimonials** - Video testimonials are considered even more powerful than a written version, given they can be seen and heard. Why not encourage customers to record a 'selfie testimonial'? Alternatively, you could record these videos yourself or make videos of yourself reading out written testimonials.

- **Reviews** - Help to strengthen your reputation by referring to 3rd-party review sites such as Google, TripAdvisor, Feefo, Freeindex, Trust Pilot etc. It's a great way to increase your exposure and engagement.

- **Recent work** - Share examples of your recent work, showcase unique projects, prestigious projects, milestone projects, exciting projects, big projects, etc. Help your customers to visualise what their project will look like with contrasting before and after photos.

- **Most popular products** - People love to know what products other people have chosen or find most popular, so why not share this information with them? E.g. *this product is perfect for X, best sellers, over 1000 sales of X, often bought together, best-rated,* etc.
- **Customer Of The Month** - Why not introduce a Customer Of The Month contest, this could include photos, quotes and reasons why they have been chosen. Winners could be selected at random or chosen strategically to build relationships or promote a successful project. Other variations could include project/makeover/achievement of the month.
- **Awards** - Awards can be an extremely powerful way of demonstrating your credentials. Why not share photos of awards that you have entered, won or even became a finalist for? Furthermore, you can share anniversaries of winning awards, showcase how these awards have benefitted/changed your business, mention the award providers for increased engagement.

7. Photos

Photos, images and diagrams are the best way to get your social media posts noticed on social networks. It's important to keep a regular supply of photos and images for your content creator.

- **Staff profile photos** - Sharing profiles of your staff either periodically or when they first join the company, helps your customers to feel a personal connection with your team. This could also be a great opportunity to display your personality and sense of humour.
- **Social events** - Let your customers see your staff in real-life work environments and help create a personal feel and connection with your company. This could include nights out, team building, fun events and other excellent achievements.
- **Staff hard at work** - Share photos of staff in a working environment, standing proud with completed projects, behind the scenes, hidden parts of the process, reveal key things about how you work or use photos to demonstrate ethical practices.
- **Customer photos** - Share photos taken alongside customers, or with custom-

ers enjoying the benefit of your products and services. You could also ask customers to send you photos of themselves doing cool and exciting events or charity work you can promote.

- **Funny captions** - Everybody likes to see funny and entertaining posts. Get your team to take existing photos and add funny captions or catchphrases.

- **Proud achievements** - Shout about the things you are proud of, they could be major business changing successes, right through to smaller achievements that are worthy of some recognition.

- **Product photos** - Professionally taken product photos will help to repeatedly maximise the desire for your products or services. Share high-quality photos from either your suppliers or manufacturers or even have some commissioned yourself by a professional photographer.

- **Product videos** - These could be provided by the manufacturer, or could be filmed after your work has been completed. Add an extra level of professionalism with a voice-over talking the viewer through the benefits.

- **Before/after photos** - Before and after photos are excellent for illustrating the kind of results your product or service can achieve when completed.

8. Interaction Posts

Posts which are renowned for getting the highest levels of engagement are ones which call on the reader to get involved and share their opinion, rather than just listen to what is being said.

- **Social polls (Facebook and Twitter)** - Social polls are quick and easy ways for you to collect valuable information from your followers in the form of a vote. Polls can be ran on Facebook and Twitter and can cover a variety of topics including current affairs, common problems, opinions about service providers and preferred values, or even something completely random and unrelated.

- **Ask a question** - As an expert in your industry, you'll no doubt already know the questions or objections your customers are likely to raise. Why not ask questions which will position your product or service in a positive light? This could be related to products/services, common problems or something completely unrelated. E.g. "When it comes to choosing a plumber what do you value the most?"

- **Fill in the blanks** - Propose a question or open-ended statement by having a section of 'blanks' where the reader can insert and voice their opinions. This is a slightly different take but has a similar effect to the 'Ask a question' post, where the customer is in the spotlight. This could include posts about common problems, values, current affairs or again, something completely unrelated to your industry. E.g. "____ is most important to me when choosing a plumber".

- **Reviews/testimonial requests** - Social media can be a great place to get some positive feedback about your work. Ask customers to comment directly or go to a form where the customer can leave feedback. You can also use 3rd-party review websites and even offer an incentive for any reviews provided.

- **Truth or fiction** - People are intrigued to learn new and interesting information. Truth or fiction is where you make a comment and invite the reader to guess if your statement is true or false. You can then follow up the post with the answer after people have been guessing. Why not state popular facts or myths relating to your business in a fun manner which actively encourages people to get involved. E.g. "Over 80% of washing machines can be repaired on the first visit, true or false?"

Tools And Software

Improving your social media productivity is a great way to ensure that you are getting the very most from your investment. It can not only be very time consuming but almost impossible to find time each and every day to think about what to post, let alone remembering to do so.

There are a number of freely available tools which can make life much easier by allowing you to upload pre-written posts to be sent out at specified times. This means that you can create your posts in a given block of time and not have to worry about them again until next month.

The software we would recommend would be Hootsuite or Buffer, they both allow for scheduling posts in advance.

Follower Engagement

By this point, you now have a very clear understanding of how to create meaningful and engaging content that your followers will be interested in. However, it's critical to remember that social media is not simply a one-way platform, it's a two-way conversation.

In order to continue growing your following, and building some goodwill within your community, here are a few things that you can do:

- Follow and like other people such as potential customers, potential partners and associates.
- Share and comment on their content if appropriate.
- Run some paid adverts to reach new prospects and encourage the growth of your followers.

CHAPTER 12

Traffic
Step 6. Blogging

The way that your customers buy from businesses has changed, people are more informed than ever before. They have a great wealth of information at their fingertips in the form of the internet. So rather than blindly accepting decisions, consumers are often already armed with vital information before they even get in touch with you.

This is a great opportunity to get an advantage, build your own credibility and engage with consumers earlier on in the buying process. Educating your customers can help them to feel empowered, but also encourage them to see things from your perspective, which in turn will ultimately have a positive effect on your sales.

Blogging is one of those things that most people realise they should be doing, but either can't find the time to dedicate to doing a professional job, or quite frankly don't actually know where or how to start. Even if you are able to start, there's the whole fear of whether your opinions are 'good enough' to be published on the internet, and how it is likely to be received when the spotlight is shining on you.

Blogging, or content marketing as it is also known, is one of the fastest growing types of online marketing with more and more businesses recognising the importance of starting to publish.

As with most areas of your local marketing system, achieving success with blogging is about following a proven formula and building it into a wider strategic plan for your business.

What Is Blogging?

The word 'blog' originates from the term 'weblog' from which it was shortened. Think of blogging as the process of publishing articles on your website. These articles are similar in format to ones you might find on news websites such as the BBC or any other newspaper or magazine.

Like an article you might see in a newspaper, they are written by an individual person, not a company or a business. This means blogs tend to have a more personal feel where the writing style is more reflective of the author's personality.

Unlike standard landing pages on your website, blog posts tend to have a published date, author credit and can allow your readers to engage by sharing them with their friends or by adding comments.

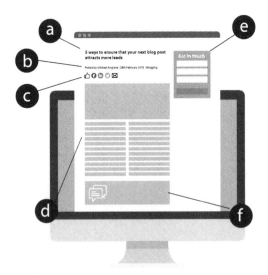

- **a) Blog post title** - A compelling title for your post which is worthy of grabbing your prospect's attention.
- **b) Publishing data** - Basic details including date published, post author, category, etc.
- **c) Sharing buttons** - A quick and easy way to encourage your readers to

share the post via social networks.

- **d) Body content** - Informative and engaging content written to educate the reader. Could also include images, diagrams, videos to help keep the reader's interest.
- **e) Data capture** - Opportunity to collect your reader's contact details on each blog post.
- **f) Comments** - Built-in facility for your readers to share opinions on your content.

Benefits Of Blogging

- **Educate and engage your customers** - Reach customers whilst they are at the research stage of the buying process and educate them about the benefits of your product.
- **Position yourself as an industry leader** - Position you and your business as a true expert in an age where web-savvy customers are doing more research than ever before.
- **Consistent and long-term leads** - Enjoy the lead generating benefits of your blog posts for months and even years to come, without spending another penny on the post.
- **Attract links to help SEO** - Blogs are more engaging, educational and are more likely to be shared than your standard sales landing pages. This makes it more likely that people will share or link to your blog post, which in turn will aid the SEO (Search Engine Optimisation) part of your local marketing system.
- **Higher converting pages** - Blog posts are usually very focused on a particular item or niche, which means they are hyper-related to the subject matter someone is searching for. Naturally, these pages can convert at a higher rate than other traffic sources.
- **Fully trackable return on investment** - Like all aspects of your local marketing system, blogging is 100% trackable when it comes to finding out how many leads each post has generated.

4 Types Of Blog Post

When it comes to creating blog posts for your website, we've identified four key types. These types are based more on their purpose within your local marketing system and have different ways in which they can help to increase the return from your blogging investment.

Traffic

Traffic posts are written with the sole purpose of looking to attract pockets of meaningful niche traffic from search engines. These keywords might have a search volume too small to justify a full-blown SEO campaign but are still likely to drive potential leads into your business.

An example of a traffic post would be "Pet friendly hotels in Liverpool" where the keyword "pet friendly hotel liverpool" has a monthly search volume of 90 searches per month. By creating a post which is centred around this subject, your post will potentially appear in search results and have a great opportunity to persuade dog owners to get in touch.

Educate & Engage

These posts are written to educate the reader and get them thinking from your perspective. They could talk about problems, features, benefits or objections which the reader may be experiencing and can help to share useful and expert knowledge. Educate and engage posts should support your sales message and can still support your SEO campaign. An example would be "7 things to ask a builder before hiring one". Although there is no search volume for this term, it will certainly add value to your sales process, as it can help to highlight and promote desirable qualities that the customer may not be aware of.

News & Events

From time to time, it may be beneficial to share latest company news with your customers and subscribers. This could be particular achievements or important customer updates that people should be aware of. These posts help to maintain a personal relationship with your customers and help them to feel part of your journey as a business.

Blog Post Extension

As part of the blogging process, you should be closely monitoring the performance of your blog over the duration of your campaign. As with all aspects of marketing and indeed business, some posts will perform better than others. You may choose to revisit a successful post in order to further increase the amount of content and value. This can further enhance the performance and drive even more leads into the business. Your effort for this post type could be to go deeper on certain sections of the post or add more details, data or images.

Coming Up With Posts Subjects And Ideas

As with most creative aspects of the local marketing system, it's always useful to have a starting point for coming up with ideas. Here are some of the best ways to get started:

- **Keyword data** - You can always use the keyword research ideas we've talked about in both the Google Ads and SEO components of the book. This data will help you to find keywords or phrases which people are actively typing into search engines.
- **Common sales objections** - Speak with your sales team and identify the most common objections they receive from new prospects. This could be a great way to create content that resonates with what's being thought in your reader's mind.
- **Common questions** - Another great way to think of ideas, is to think about the questions that you receive in real life from your customers. If you hear the same questions over and over, these can be great ways to identify potentially valuable subjects.
- **Talk to your customers** - If you are unsure of potential blog post ideas,

why not speak to your customers and ask them directly. This could also be done online using a survey containing either open-ended or multiple choice questions.

- **Generate potential questions using software** - There are two great free tools which are called Askthepublic.com and keywordtool.io. Both of these tools allow you to enter your main keywords and automatically generate a list of questions which are related to the subject.
- **Copy what has worked for others** - If in doubt, look to your competitors around the world and see what they are blogging about. Once you've identified subjects, you can recreate this content in your own style with your own slant on the topic.
- **Find questions on social media** - Social media is arguably the best place to hear conversations happening, so why not search for your keywords in order to get a gist for the kind of subjects that are getting people talking. The best social networks to start with would be Twitter, Quora, and Reddit.
- **Create sub-categories for existing posts** - If you have popular posts already, then why not try breaking them down into further sub-topics. This can help to elaborate more on particular markets, subjects or niches.

How To Write Great Blog Posts

So now you've identified the perfect subject for your blog posts, the next step is to write the post itself. Now there's no set structure or style to use when writing blog posts, but there are a number of best practices that we've identified, to help you create great content:

- **Conduct subject research** - If you ask any professional writer, the secret to creating great content is often in the preparation conducted beforehand. Allocate time for reading about the subject online or in magazines, this can help to ensure that your article is well thought through and clearly structured. Even if you're writing content based on your experience, it's always advisable to create a plan to ensure your post is concise and 'waffle' free.
- **Be conversational** - Remember blog posts are written by people, not by organisations or companies. Keep your writing style conversational where possible as if it has been written by an individual person. This will help your

reader to build a stronger connection with the author.

- **Use images and visual content** - Nothing is more daunting to a reader than huge blocks of text. It looks scary and feels like it will take a long time to read. Using images within your posts will help to keep your reader's attention and can also help to convey ideas, statistics and more.
- **Use short paragraphs and lists** - Don't necessarily look at how long a post should be, or aim for an exact word count, but make it more about being interesting and useful. The blog post can never be too long, it can only be too boring. Break your post into smaller paragraphs of no more than 4 or 5 lines, use bullet point lists to keep the content snappy and help maintain the reader's interest.
- **Dual-readership path** - Many people who read blog posts, actually don't read them in full. They land on the page and quickly scan the article to see if it looks like something they would be interested in reading in full. The dual-readership path means that scan readers should also be able to get the gist of the article before deciding whether or not to read in full. This can be achieved by using meaningful headings, sub-headings, lists and images with captions.
- **Use stories** - Stories are one of the most effective ways to keep the attention of the human brain. Rather than share technical details or listing features, why not give an example using powerful imagery and involving characters. Our brains are more able to retain stories over factual content.
- **Use statistics** - Statistics in the form of numbers will stand out from your page and can really help to convey your ideas. When using statistics, it's also powerful to back up the credibility of your numbers by citing the source.
- **Cross-sell your services and offers** - Be sparing with this, but include links to other key pages or advertise your lead magnet where possible. By this stage, you've worked hard to get the reader's attention, it would be a shame to miss out on the opportunity to advance a sales situation.
- **Include a call to action** - Don't leave the reader hanging at the end of the article. Always make sure there is something to do next. It could be something to think about, an action to take or a web page to visit.

Getting Your Blog Post Distributed

One of the biggest mistakes when it comes to blogging is thinking that simply publishing your post will be enough to get it seen by your prospects and customers. It'd be nice if people were always thinking about your company and checking in for updates, but for the vast majority of small businesses, this sadly isn't the case.

Once your blog post has been published, it's time to get to work on the distribution phase of your system. Here are some of the most effective ways to get your new post seen quickly:

- **Email marketing** - Make a teaser email to send out to your list of email subscribers. It could have the first paragraph of the blog post to entice people to click back to your blog to continue reading. Once this has been sent out, you can always add the blog post into the automated follow-up sequence (more on this later) to ensure that future subscribers can also benefit from this content.
- **Social media** - Social is a great way to share your post with your followers. You could use teaser copy to build intrigue, or even focus on a small fact, concept or quote from the post. With social media being such a fast moving platform, don't make the mistake of sharing it once and thinking everyone has now seen it. Post it at least 3 or 4 times over the coming days or weeks. Why not share this through multiple channels such as Facebook, Twitter, LinkedIn, Google+ and more.
- **Latest posts on your website** - A great way to reach more people with your post is to display your recent articles in either the sidebar or footer of your website. This way, your general website users will be able to easily access the new content.
- **Search engines** - Getting your post quickly indexed in Google will help to build its authority and hopefully start to drive traffic for itself. If you've created a traffic post, getting it indexed quickly is crucial. This can be done by regularly submitting your sitemap to Google's Search Console or by adding your latest posts to every page on your website. This is a great way to get Google's search bot to notice the new post when it visits your strongest pages, such as your homepage.

CHAPTER 13

Re-Engagement
Step 7. Facebook Ads

So now we move into the next phase of the system, Re-engagement. Each component covered in this section will be utilised to continue marketing to your prospects long after they've left your website. The first stage of this process is using Facebook ads.

It's no secret how popular and powerful Facebook has become in today's world. A whopping 78% of over 18-year-olds in the UK have an active Facebook account with a large proportion of those using the platform on a daily basis.

With such a huge number of regular users, this surely has to be a great opportunity for your business to reach people and make some money. You may have heard stories about businesses which have been getting incredible results and wondered if this could be possible for you too.

Perhaps you've already given it a go but struggled to get it working like you had hoped, leaving you burning through your budget without getting anything in return? You no doubt saw the data of how many people you were reaching, but it's likely that it didn't result in an increase in leads or more importantly profit.

Simply put, Facebook Advertising isn't a one-size fits all solution. Although it can work effectively for almost any business, there are some extremely important differences depending on the type of products and services you sell. However, before you dive in headfirst, you need to make sure you understand what you're dealing with and how you can develop a strategy that works for you today and well into the future.

What Is Facebook Advertising?

When you become an advertiser, you can buy promotional space in various places on their platform and mobile apps, including Instagram and other 3rd-party apps. These can be shown in your news feed or other designated areas.

Adverts can be shown to users based on any number of factors including demographics, interests, locations, financial background or previous engagement with your company page, posts or website. Adverts can be created in various sizes and can take the form of text, photos and videos.

Furthermore, you can also control exactly how you choose to pay for your adverts. This can be based on the number of people you reach or the number of clicks or conversions you receive.

Benefits Of Facebook Ads

- **The biggest pool of potential customers** - Facebook has the largest number of active users of any social network. This means a large proportion of your potential customers are using it, regardless of your industry or if you sell business to business.
- **Customise your target audience** - Reach people based on specific targeting. You can advertise to people by age, interests, behaviours, location, income, friends and much more.
- **Adverts live within minutes** - One of the fastest routes to generating traffic available in the world. Once your ads are set to live and approved by Facebook, you can start receiving clicks and potentially enquiries and sales within minutes.
- **Fully trackable return on investment** - Like all aspects of your local marketing system, Facebook is 100% trackable when it comes to working out your return on investment.
- **Re-engage existing customers** - Your content will often be seen by existing customers. They can not only reconnect for further sales, they can also help to build social validation by liking, sharing and commenting on your posts.

- **Grow your follower base** - When you promote useful content to your ideal audience, you will naturally begin to pick up new followers to your page along the way.

Re-Engagement Campaign Types

There are a number of different campaign strategies which can be used to your advantage. Understanding the key differences and choosing the most suitable campaign will be imperative to your success. We've outlined four campaign types along with their pros and cons to help you figure out the best place to get started.

1. Retargeting Website Visitors

Now that you're getting traffic from search engines, retargeting is a perfect way to 'remarket' to people who have recently been on your website, but not yet completed your goal.

Installing the Facebook Pixel means that whenever someone lands on your website, if Facebook can detect an active Facebook account, it will add them to a custom audience list which can then be used as a target audience to display your ads to.

Not only can you build an audience of website visitors, you can also tailor this audience depending on a number of factors. This could include the specific pages they have visited, their interests or other demographic data.

Pros

Retargeting is extremely cost effective by only showing your ads to people who have engaged with your website. People who recognise your adverts are more likely to re-engage or click as they are familiar with your page and offer. It's surprising how many people don't take action right away, so this is a great way to recapture those who may have procrastinated first time around.

Cons

This type of campaign will only work if you are currently driving traffic to your website from other areas.

2. Targeting Email Lists

This type of campaign is very similar to retargeting campaigns, but instead, it will allow you to show ads to your existing email subscribers. Facebook will allow you to import a list of contacts from your CRM or email software. This could be people who have opted-in to receive your marketing or even a list of existing customers for whom you have permission to market to.

Pros

This is a great way to quickly get started with a high impact Facebook ads campaign, reaching proven customers in a cost-effective manner.

As these are prospects and customers you have already engaged with, they are likely to be familiar with your company, making it a great way to reconnect.

Cons

You may face issues if people's email addresses don't match those used on their Facebook accounts. This is particularly relevant if your company markets to businesses or professional users as they rarely use work email addresses to sign up for Facebook. You must have a freshly opted-in list of contacts for whom you have received permission to market to.

3. Lookalike Audiences

If you currently have an audience which is being used for your Facebook ads, then you can use this audience as a mould for finding new people who Facebook deems to be similar in their interests, demographics and most importantly, the likelihood that they'll also complete the same goal (e.g. make a purchase or submit an enquiry).

Although this may initially appear to be similar to targeting, it actually relies on

Facebook's own algorithm which is significantly more sophisticated at predicting similar users than standard targeting options. This could include posts and pages that they've liked, shared or even read in the past.

Pros

Great for scaling an already profitable campaign by utilising Facebook's intelligence for finding more potential customers.

Cons

You will need an engaged and proven audience before you implement this into your campaign.

4. Targeting

Before we start with this, it's worth noting that we're now in the re-engagement section, and targeting isn't re-engagement, it technically falls into the traffic section. However targeting is the most commonly used model for businesses using Facebook ads, so it's important to cover this to ensure that you understand the difference.

As the name suggests, this campaign will allow you to show your ads to Facebook users based on any given set of criteria. Facebook has a huge range of criteria by which you can filter individual users, covering the following and more:

- Age
- Gender
- Marital status
- Location
- Income / net worth
- Interests
- Pages or people they 'like' or engage with

Although this sounds fantastic and may make your eyes water at the thought of all of those potential new customers, it's not just about reaching people. It's actually about generating a return on your investment, which is extremely dependent on how compelling your 'offer' is. We'll cover this later on.

Pros

You can reach a huge number of people very quickly and easily with a comprehensive set of targeting parameters.

Campaigns can be set up quickly and can result in 'instant' traffic to your website.

Getting this running smoothly requires well-defined and easily identifiable interest groups, such as business owners, fitness fanatics, parents of young children, mountain climbers, musicians etc.

Cons

The biggest downside of targeting campaigns for many small businesses is the difficulty in identifying who is ready to buy. Let's take for example a building company. It's certainly possible to identify homeowners of a particular age group in an affluent location. But that doesn't necessarily mean they are looking to have their house extended. This may, in turn, result in spending lots of money to show ads to everyone in order to just reach a smaller group who are in the market to buy.

This is why retargeting to people who have recently been searching for 'house extensions' or 'building company', and have actually already been on your website demonstrates clear buying intent.

That said, if your product has a high-ticket price with a large average order value, you may still be able to make the numbers work with this method.

Secondly, people aren't looking to buy when using Facebook, so it can be difficult to get engagement if you are trying to sell. You also run the risk of appearing like the annoying pest, or worse, having your ads ignored altogether. You will need to continually refresh your ads, to avoid them losing effectiveness.

The more users who see your ads, the more they begin to 'fatigue' over time. Once users start to ignore your ads, Facebook naturally shows them less, making it difficult to reach your goals.

Getting Started With Facebook Ads

Selling V Engagement

Facebook and other social media channels have a distinct difference over search engines, in that Facebook users are not actively looking to buy your products and services. Facebook users are there to interact and socialise with their friends.

Given this important truth, we recommend you split your monthly ad budget into two parts, 80% of the budget for selling and directly trying to attract new leads into your business, and the remaining 20% for engaging with your audience by promoting or boosting organic content.

This approach helps to 'warm up' the audience with interesting content and also helps to break up the number of adverts they see, and therefore reducing the risk of people hiding future communications from your business.

Structuring Your Campaign

Before we get started with setting up your Facebook ads campaign, I'd like to begin by covering some of the basic components you will encounter. The whole structure for Facebook ads is not a million miles away from Google Ads as you will see.

Campaigns

Like with Google Ads, campaigns are your top-level way of categorising your adverts and can be used to group your products, services, locations, niches or even by your campaign objective or type.

Ad Sets

Ad Sets are similar to ad groups in Google Ads and are used to group sets of ads which are closely related. Unlike Google Ads, daily budget limits can be configured at ad set and campaign level.

Adverts

Adverts are the copywriting, images and videos that the end-user will ultimately see when browsing Facebook.

Pixel Tracking Code

The way that Facebook is able to collect data for you to use in your retargeting campaign is through it's tracking pixel. The vast majority of Facebook users will be continuously signed into their account, even if they haven't visited Facebook recently. This means that when a pixel detects an active account, it will be associated with any website pages they have viewed. Each time a page on your website is loaded, the pixel is able to record this information.

Tip: Whether you intend to get started with Facebook ads right away, or you're going to wait for a few months, I would strongly recommend that you get this added to your website as soon as possible. This way you can start to benefit from building your audience data in preparation for your future campaign.

The pixel is simply a snippet of code which can be added to your website by your website developer or added using a plugin if you use Wordpress. The plugin we would recommend is called Pixel Caffeine and can be installed for free.

Tip: Make sure you check whether or not the pixel is actually tracking once the pixel code is installed. This can be done using the official Facebook pixel browser extension for Google Chrome.

Conversion Tracking

Being able to track how many of your clicks turned into actual leads is probably one of the most important metrics you'll need to monitor. So be sure to get this in place before spending a single penny on advertising. Once your pixel is installed and tracking correctly, setting up conversion tracking is a pretty straightforward process.

Conversions can be set to trigger when a particular page URL has been reached, such as a thank you page. A conversion can also be triggered on an event such as a download button or a telephone 'click to call'.

Audience Configuration

When it comes to Facebook, an audience is basically a way of grouping users. Audiences can be created based on demographic attributes, like their age, gender, interests, or their behavioural activities, like which websites they've visited or which Facebook pages they have liked.

Do not underestimate the power of your audience in your search for success. Earlier on in the book we talked about market, message and media. Well, your audience in this situation is your market. Being prepared to closely track and optimise your audience will mean that you can maintain a profitable collection of prospects.

Recording and Segmenting Users

So far you've been able to drive searchers to your website, but the majority of them will not yet have completed a marketing goal. So whilst you're recording your audience you're now able to continue to reach them by showing them your adverts.

Audiences can be created by building particular conditions such as *people who visited X website address*. For example, a plumber may want to record a different audience for people who looked at *boiler servicing* to those who looked at the *emergency call outs* page. It's worth noting that it's also possible to exclude particular pages too, helping you to narrow down your audience.

It's critical to build a separate 'converters' audience in order to remove visitors who have successfully completed a goal. This will ensure that you are not wasting money by paying again to reach people who have already taken action.

Furthermore, and as an advanced technique, you may also be able to promote the next step in your marketing system. For example, if your initial goal is to get people to request a copy of your lead magnet. The second goal might be to get them to book an initial consultation meeting. You could create a campaign specifically designed to advertise the benefits of attending.

As we've already mentioned in the campaign types, it's also possible to upload a list of emails which can then be turned into an audience. The success of this depends on the email address you have stored, matching with the email connected to the user's Facebook account.

So far we've talked about audiences which we can build ourselves. There is also a feature to allow Facebook to create an audience on your behalf based on its data and artificial intelligence. This is how we can build the lookalike campaigns previously mentioned.

Ad Placement

If you're a regular Facebook user, you'll no doubt already know that Facebook allows adverts to be positioned in several different positions on the website or on their app. Each one of these positions is called a placement. As you might expect, the placement of the ad can make a huge difference to how effective the ad is in terms of generating conversions.

Here is a breakdown of the main placements and how they might be beneficial to your campaign.

News feed - These are the most popular type of ads, as they generally get the most attention. These ads are created to look similar to organic posts and will appear in the main news feed along with posts from friends and other profiles that the user has engaged with.

Right column - The right-hand column is only available on desktop computers like laptops and will allow you to show your ads in this small condensed placement.

Instant Articles - Instant Articles are Facebook's super fast loading pages designed to allow news publishers to distribute their articles for fast consumption. Your adverts can be placed to appear midway through these articles.

In-stream video (video only) - If you're running video adverts, you can utilise the in-stream placement which means your video will appear midway through other video content which is currently being viewed by the user and can even be shown during Facebook Live broadcasts.

Marketplace - Facebook Marketplace is an environment which has been designed for people looking to sell products to users. Marketplace ads will be shown as users browse this e-commerce platform.

Instagram feeds - Since Facebook's acquisition of Instagram, the advertising platforms have been cleverly integrated, meaning getting your adverts to appear on Instagram is as simple as selecting this placement. Choose this placement to get your adverts positioned in Instagram's very popular main news feed.

Instagram stories - Instagram stories are very much like Snapchat stories in that the user's posts will disappear after a 24 hour period. You can show your adverts whilst users are browsing Instagram stories.

Messenger home - Messenger is a mobile app designed to improve the experience and speed at which Facebook users can send text, voice or video messages for free. Your ads will appear whilst the user is operating within the main home screen of the app.

Sponsored messages - The sponsored message placement allows you to display your ads neatly in between actual conversations and messages from friends.

Audience network - The audience network is much greater than just the core Facebook apps and can extend to any number of 3rd-party websites, mobile apps and even TV apps which have integrated the functionality.

Best Place To Start With Placements

Now that you're clear on all of the different placements available, it's easy to think that you should show you advert across all of them. However, the best starting place is to create your ads just to appear on the main news feed of Facebook. Once you're able to figure out what works best for generating more leads, then start to experiment with other placements. This will give you the clearest indicators of which placements are working best for your market and message.

Relevancy Score

The secret to getting ads which not only work best but cost the least is to ensure that your content is closely related to what interests the user. Relevancy score is similar to the way quality score works with Google Ads, in that a score ranging from 1-10 is allocated for each advert in your ad set. Not only will this help you to interpret how your ads are performing, it will ultimately have an impact on how much you pay for each click.

Scores are calculated automatically based on the feedback and interaction they receive from the user. Any users who see your advert can act either positively (positive reactions, comment, share, click your call to action, watch your video, etc.) or negatively (negative reaction, ignore it, hide it, report it, etc.). The more positivity, the higher the relevancy score.

Relevancy score will only be calculated for your adverts once it has been seen 500 times, and scores can change over time. If your relevancy score begins to drop, it's an indicator that your advert might be starting to fatigue, and may need refreshing.

Choosing Images

Given the fast-moving nature of Facebook, the biggest challenge is getting that initial burst of attention to capture the readers' eye. The most powerful component for achieving this is the imagery you use. Research shows that it's the image or video which often first attracts the focus of the eye.

Your success in this area will depend on your ability to be able to quickly test lots of new images rather than your ability to choose the perfect image. You need to regularly and systematically try out new images and advert design styles for your adverts in order to let the market decide which works best.

When it comes to choosing images, there are four key categories you can get started with:

1. **Product images** - These could be images of the products you sell or photos which relate to the services being completed. For example, it could feature a plumber fixing a tap, or a mechanic examining a car or website developer writing code.

2. **Benefit images** - These would represent the benefit that the customer receives as a consequence of buying your product or service. For example, someone drinking a refreshing glass of water from the recently fixed tap, someone happily driving their car after it has been repaired, or a business owner speaking to new customers now the leads are coming in from the website.

3. **Problem images** - Every product in business either takes away a problem or adds pleasure. This is a great chance to use images which help to convey the problem they are currently experiencing. It could be a sense of frustration, stress, worry or even actual pain depending on the products or services which you provide.

4. **Value proposition** - These images would show your value proposition directly. If you're offering a free downloadable guide, then you could show a mockup. If you're offering free coupons, then show a coupon, if you're offering a free appraisal show photos of one in action, etc.

Here are some further tips when it comes to choosing images for each of the above categories:

- **Represent your target market** - These images should depict the demographic of the customer you are looking to attract, including age, gender, family situation, income, or a specific niche you are targeting. Remember, by this stage you will have already identified a clear image of your customer along with an emotional profile of what makes them tick!
- **Real images will work best** - Real images of real people tend to help convey truth and believability in your marketing. If real images are out of the question, then use stock images as a secondary option.
- **Use images of people** - It's human nature for our eyes to be immediately drawn to other human eyes. Even the direction of where people are looking can be important. Imagine walking into a room full of people, where do you think your eyes would be drawn first, the people looking and talking to each other, or the person staring directly at you? Further to this, if the person is looking at something, you will be more inclined to follow their line of sight. This can be used to your advantage if the subject of the photo is looking at some important text or in the direction of your call to action button.
- **Stand out from the crowd** - There are no specific types of images that always perform best and in some ways, simply doing something different to your competitors can be the best thing to do. If all of your competitors are running professional images of people in a home, it might be worth testing an image of a cartoon, remember the initial aim is to get your advert noticed.
- **Keep your images relevant** - I know I talked about standing out from the crowd, but remember your images must be relevant to the context of your advert and offer. Yes, you may be able to 'shock' the reader to get their attention, but unless you can tie that back to your offer, you'll lose their focus as quickly as you got it.
- **Test images often and regularly** - Rather than try to guess what the perfect image might be, plan to test many of them and quickly. This means you'll be able to get actual data to prove which one is best.
- **Use the same image on your landing page** - Once you've started to identify the highest impact images, try also including them on your landing page. This helps to build consistency when navigating between Facebook and your

website.

- **Rotate images regularly** - Failure to regularly rotate and test new images can result in 'ad fatigue' and will increase the risk of users becoming resistant to your adverts or worse yet, blocking them from displaying in the future.

Advert Copywriting

Just like with any Advert, as soon as you have the reader's attention, the copy in your headline will be critical in helping them to assess whether this is something they should keep reading or discard.

Many of the advert copywriting techniques we've already talked about on pages 68-69 will also apply when it comes to creating adverts for Facebook:

- Speak in your customer's language
- Benefits first, features second
- Don't go over the top with hype
- Use social proof to back up your claims
- Use a compelling call to action to encourage an immediate response
- Check spelling and grammar in your adverts for the best first impression

However, there are also some slight nuances which you may need to be aware of:

- **Keep your advert relevant to the original keyword used or pages they originally visited** - Remember with retargeting, we're only showing your advert to people who have been on your website already. They most likely arrived because they were searching for a company to help solve a problem. Ensure your advert is related to that original search query.
- **People aren't naturally in buying mode** - Facebook is slightly different to search adverts in the sense that people aren't on Facebook at that instance in order to buy. Now that's not to say that they can't be tempted back to your website to continue the sales process. For this reason, it could be worth testing a more educational and problem-solving approach to your adverts. This could include a post describing the best way to solve a particular problem. For example, *7 Ways To Increase The Value Of Your House.*

Video Adverts

It's worth noting that one of the most effective ways to get potential customers to see your sales message on Facebook, is with video. Recording your sales message either in person or using a slideshow style video with a voiceover can be a great way to keep your readers' attention without leaving Facebook.

Facebook ads can just as easily be created using videos as they can with images, yet they are proven to capture and retain attention longer than text or images.

Creating video isn't easy and may require you or your team to step outside of your comfort zone to start with, but when your future success is at stake, it's certainly worth giving it a try.

It might be tempting to hire a company to make you a flashy professional video. However, in our experience, we'd recommend putting together something yourself first to make sure your script and sales message work before committing to an expensive production.

Here's a quick and simple way to test a video in a matter of hours without breaking the bank.

Slideshow Video

Slideshow videos are the quickest and easiest videos to get you started. A slideshow video is pretty much what it says on the tin. It's a slideshow presentation like you would create in Powerpoint or Google Slides, with a voiceover playing over the top. Not only can you produce a video like this in a matter of hours, it's the perfect choice if you're feeling camera shy.

1. Start by writing your video script. Be sure to talk about the problems you are able to help your prospect overcome and remember to clearly define your unique selling proposition.

2. Print out the script and read it aloud, this will help you to get a feel for what it sounds like in spoken word.

3. If you have an iPhone, open up the Voice recorder app (I'm sure you can download something similar for other platforms) and confidently read your script with a good level of energy. It's much easier if you're able to record it in a single take, but if you're comfortable editing audio, then feel free to do so.

4. Next, you'll need to create your presentation, just as you would if you were tasked with making a powerpoint presentation. Keep it short and to the point, and use text to highlight key points as you talk through them. You might also want to use some subtle fading animations as it will help to keep the attention of more visual learners.

5. The last stage is the most tricky, however with a little practice, you can soon get something together. You will need to start recording your screen and put your Powerpoint into full-screen mode. Then start playback of your audio recording you just created on your phone. As the audio plays, you click your mouse or the keyboard arrows toggle each relevant slide. Whilst you are doing this, your screen will be recorded by your software. For recording your screen, I would recommend a program called Camtasia which is a paid piece of software. For a free alternative, try iSpring Free Cam available for both Mac and Windows.

6. Now you've recorded your video, you'll need to send the audio recording from your phone to your email account. This will allow you to import the high quality MP3 file into your screen recording software. You may need to trim any excess footage at the beginning or end before exporting the video ready for uploading to Facebook.

If this all feels a little daunting, then delegate the task to someone in your team or outsource it.

Move On To Video

We've always believed in getting something going as soon as possible, so if you're not ready to record a video then get started with standard ads. They can always help you to test and refine your message to ensure that you're already on your way to having a winning formula by the time you get around to producing your video.

Management & Optimisation

Without wanting to sound like a broken record, I'm going to bang on about testing once more. As with all components of your local marketing system, the secret to mastering your Facebook ads is to be continually testing everything.

We'll be covering split testing in more detail in step 10, but until then, here are a few tips to get you moving:

1. **Commit to regularly checking your account** - Ensuring that you are regularly checking your account and running new tests in a systematic fashion will be the only way to ensure that your results are getting better.
2. **Test your placements** - The placement of your ads will make a significant difference to how well each one performs. Once you're happy with your advert in your news feed, gradually start testing other placements one at a time with the same ad. This will give you intelligence of which placements might be viable and which ones aren't.
3. **Test your images** - As we've already established in this chapter, images (and videos) will prove to be one of the most important components of your campaign. It's critical that you keep testing. If your best images start to gradually become less effective, then try playing around with them including, re-cropping, applying filters, image effects and text overlays to re-invigorate them with some extra energy.
4. **Speed up your website landing pages** - We notice a significant drop-off when customers go from Facebook to a slow landing page. The longer your page takes to load, the higher your drop-off for users losing patience and interest. Do whatever you can to increase the speed of your website.
5. **In fact... test everything** - This really goes without saying, Facebook is getting increasingly more competitive and your ability to increase performance and lower costs could be the difference between winning and losing over the coming months and years.

CHAPTER 14

Re-Engagement
Step 8. Automated Follow-up

For many business owners, following up on leads is probably one of the least glamorous and most tedious parts of your sales and marketing, yet at the same time, one of the most important when it comes to impact on your profitability.

For most business owners, there are many jobs that you have to become accustomed to doing, whether you like it or not. Jobs which may even initially lie outside of your comfort zone. For many, following up on leads is one of those things.

Whether it's yourself or your sales team, replying to that initial enquiry is exciting! No doubt you're quick to get across your initial information or to arrange your initial meeting in the hope of winning a new customer.

However, things become less exciting when that person hasn't got back to you or is just 'thinking about' your proposal. It's at this point that 80% of businesses stop following up on that lead and move on to the next one.

According to studies, many sales teams report 6-8 contact touches before a customer is ready to proceed with a sale. Not surprisingly, this number is only likely to rise given the buying trends of people spending longer researching and putting off important buying decisions.

Most people give up because this is where it starts to get uncomfortable. It's hard to think of different reasons for your call, and you start to feel like an annoyance. To be frank, it feels like there are more important things on which you can spend your time.

If there aren't at least eight follow-up points in your sales system, then ultimately you're going to be missing out on potential revenue. Considering you've already invested money and time into getting this lead, what do you really have to lose?

According to data recorded by email provider Adestra, 61% of users in 2017 opened their emails on their smartphone. With the mobile usage at its highest ever level, email remains one of the fastest and most efficient ways to reach your customers and prospects, at any time of the day.

Email is undoubtedly a fantastic opportunity as it's quick, easy and super affordable for literally any business. However, as with most things that are easy, it usually means more people are already doing it, and it's getting increasingly harder to get effective results.

Take a moment to think of your own email inbox. How many emails do you receive each day? If you're like most people in business, you'll be inundated with spam or irrelevant emails that you never signed up for, or have little interest in reading.

Ensuring that your email cuts through the noise and resonates with your prospects' thoughts, relies on having a powerful sequence of messages delivered at regular and consistent intervals.

Automation is the perfect solution for providing the follow-up towards the later stages when interest starts to drop, and the best part is you don't have to lift a finger. In fact, the only time you'll even realise it is happening is when someone reaches out for more information or to proceed with your proposal.

Email automation is still very new and uncommon in most small businesses, so this really is a great opportunity to maximise the impact of your local marketing system. Understanding what content to put in your follow-up sequence is often the part where people fall short.

We've been working with email automation since 2013, during which time, we've been able to learn a lot about what works and what doesn't. From this vital experience, we've been able to create proven systems in order to maximise the effectiveness and squeeze out each and every possible sale.

What Is Automated Follow-Up?

One of the core foundations of your local marketing system is capturing the contact details of your customers in order to be able to continue marketing to them long after they initially landed on your website.

When they fill out a contact form on your landing page, their contact information will be emailed to you, and also stored in an online system (platforms like MailChimp) so that you have the ability to easily send them emails in the future.

Furthermore, this will trigger a series of automated emails to be delivered to each subscriber automatically. Emails are sent individually to each subscriber and at predefined intervals (e.g. every 7 days). This means each and every subscriber passes through the same sequence, in the same order, but just at different times. Timings are calculated automatically based on the time and date the prospect signed up.

Users should always have the ability to easily unsubscribe from these emails at any point. If your prospect decided against using your business, they should be able to stop all future emails. There's absolutely no value in emailing people who do not want to receive your messages.

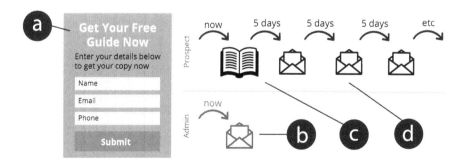

- **a) Web form is completed** - The user starts by filling out a form to receive some kind of benefit. It could be in the form to request a quote, claim a free gift or to receive free information to help their purchase.

- **b) Admin notification is sent** - On the successful completion of a web form, you will receive an email notification including their details, so that you can follow up immediately with their request.

- **c) Prospect notification is sent** - The prospect will now be automatically emailed their free information and will be informed that you will soon be in touch.

- **d) Automated email sequence begins** - From this point and at pre-defined time intervals, the prospect will now start to receive your emails, making you look proactive and keeping you fresh in their mind.

Benefits Of Automated Follow-Up

- **Building a list** - One of the most tangible benefits will come from the steady and continual growth of the list of prospects and customers, who can be reached at any time with the click of a button.

- **Squeeze out maximum sales** - At this point, each lead has already been paid for and followed up manually, so why not maximise the number of sales you could win, by continuing to follow up long after everyone else has stopped.

- **No ongoing time investment** - Other than the setup time and the ongoing optimisation for improvements, automated follow-up requires no time investment on an operational level, other than replying to messages that you receive.

- **Starts to work within weeks** - Once the campaign is running, all subscribers will start to receive your automated emails meaning this can have an impact on your bottom line quickly.

- **You look proactive and organised** - For those who simply haven't got round to making a decision yet, your emails will act as a gentle reminder that you are still there and waiting to help. Remember, many of your competitors haven't even bothered to follow-up at all.

Perfect Uses For Automated Follow-Up

- **Following up with 'lost leads'** - Leads that may have 'gone cold' can be contacted automatically in case their situation changes or they become ready to buy.
- **Building extra credibility** - You can build authority by demonstrating proof, sharing customer success stories, testimonials, reviews, awards, accreditations and more.
- **Educating your customers** - Help to create more informed customers by explaining the benefits of your products or services and why they are suitable.
- **Objection handling** - Answering questions and objections which commonly crop up during your sales process. Even if you've already answered them initially, this can be a great way to repeat and reiterate.
- **Keeping in touch** - Ensure that people who procrastinated during the buying decision are gently reminded of your brand, services and products.

Getting Your Automated-Follow-Up Setup

If you've never heard of automated marketing before, don't panic. It's a new concept for many business owners and offers some exciting opportunities when it comes to generating and closing new leads. Here are each of the core components along with some key pointers to help you get started quickly.

Email Software

Each and every time somebody completes a form on your website, their data should not only be emailed to you or your sales team for the usual follow-up process, but your prospects' details should be added to your Email Marketing software so that you can continue to communicate with them long after they've left your website.

The email gets added to your 'list' which naturally continues to grow each and every time an enquiry form is completed on your website. Each new contact should also be added to an automated sequence so the prospect can start receiving automatic emails.

The ease of getting automation set up and the features available vary depending on your choice of software. There are literally hundreds of different platforms to choose from, but here are some of the most popular ones which we would recommend:

- MailChimp
- ActiveCampaign
- Drip
- Campaign Monitor

Furthermore, you could alternatively use CRM (Client Relationship Manager) software. A CRM in its simplest form will store structured details about your customers. This could include their contact details and information related to their sales enquiries, right through to managing your company dashboards and sales reports.

There are a number of CRM systems which also allow you to send automated emails to these stored contacts as part of its functionality. It's outside of the scope of this book to go into any great detail here, but I'd like to list a few popular CRM systems which have automation inbuilt:

- Infusionsoft
- Hubspot
- Marketo
- Agile CRM

If you don't already have anything in place, choosing your software can be a difficult task, given the amount of choice. My advice would be to take your time and choose carefully. Be sure to try out any free demos to ensure you and your team are comfortable with how it operates.

Factors which affect price include how many emails you intend to send and how many contacts you have on your email list. If you're just starting out, I would recommend looking to minimise the stress and overheads by going with a platform like MailChimp. Not only is this ever-evolving software getting increasingly more powerful, it's also completely free until you reach 2000 contacts.

Connecting To Your Website

Getting your contacts from your web forms into your email or CRM software is the first step to putting your campaign live. If you have an existing website which currently has web forms, then it's probably best to speak to your web designer regarding integration.

Alternatively, most platforms will allow you to easily create web forms from which you can simply paste the code into your pages.

Email Design

The number of emails the average person receives today can be truly staggering and well over 100. For this reason, it's more important than ever to ensure that your emails are easily recognisable to your subscribers.

We find that the most effective way to design emails in your Automated Follow-Up sequence is to make them look and feel just like the emails you are sending on a daily basis. This means they'll recognise them as being sent from you personally. Emails which have the look and feel of personal email will statistically have a better chance of being read.

Try and replicate you or your sales team's existing email signatures. It may include your company logo, name, job title, and other key contact information.

Lead Generation Magnet

Like we've already discussed (on page 40), in order to attract the maximum number of leads into your business, you will need an 'irresistible offer', something of value to exchange for their contact information.

Your lead magnet is a perfect tool to aid the user in their pursuit to solve their problems and hopefully buy your products or services in the process.

If your lead magnet is a digital item like a downloadable PDF, coupon codes or a video, then this asset should be sent to the subscriber in the first email of your automation sequence, we'll come to how to do this shortly.

Planning Your Emails

Before you start writing anything, it's a good idea to start brainstorming the types of emails that you could include in your initial sequence. This way you're less likely to overlook important subjects which could benefit your sales funnel. Here are some of the key email types which you might want to consider adding to your sequence. Read through the examples below and start to build a list of potential email subjects.

Welcome Emails

The first email (or emails) in your sequence should be ones that welcome the new subscriber. Use this email to introduce yourself, share your mission and manage their expectations as to what they are going to receive in terms of future emails. This should explain the benefits of why they should stay tuned in to what you are sharing.

Social Proof

Social proof is one of the strongest ways to get your message across as people believe what others say about you and your products more than what you say about yourself. They'll assume (and are probably correct in doing so) that you are biased. These emails could include testimonials, case studies, reviews, awards, endorsements, key business milestone achievements etc.

Sales

It's important not to shy away from addressing key sales-related concerns which the customer may be feeling. This could range from handling frequently experienced objections, raising awareness of particular benefits and describing what makes your service unique. It could also be used to announce sales initiatives like promotions, referral schemes or even request testimonials. The best way to identify your most common objections will be to talk with your sales team directly. They'll have often already mastered how to handle these objections, so their input here will be invaluable.

Education And Information

Emails are often most interesting when there's something in it for the reader. As the expert in your field, there's a wealth of knowledge which can be tapped into to provide useful nuggets of information that will benefit them directly. These emails might include free tips, explaining how and why products work, how to overcome recently experienced problems and much more. Don't think that these emails have to be 'revolutionary' it's often the simple things which make the biggest impact with your customers. Don't fall into the trap of assuming your customers are as knowledgeable as you are when it comes to your specialist area.

Entertainment

Finally, depending on the type of business you run, it's often possible to create emails which are entertainment focused. People love to be entertained by reading about stories, anecdotes, photos or funny things that have happened in your business. These emails can provide a light-hearted relief in your sales sequence. You may be surprised at how it can help to build relationships with prospects when you uncover a little more of your personality.

I wouldn't recommend doing too many entertainment emails unless you can find a way to tie it back to a call to action. This way you won't miss out on any sales related opportunity of having the reader's attention.

Writing Your Emails

Now that you've mapped out a structure for the emails you are going to be writing, it's time to get started. Here are a few top tips for getting the most out of your automated follow-up sequences.

Top Tips For Writing Emails:

- **Use a personal look and feel** - Writing in a conversational (one-to-one) style will help to make the reader feel valued like you are talking to them directly and not lots of people at once.
- **Be interesting** - Keep your emails moving quickly, don't use unnecessary technical jargon, be short, sharp and tell stories to stop your emails becoming boring.
- **Ask questions to encourage replies** - Almost all personally sent emails will naturally engage with your recipient by asking questions and making requests. Do the same with emails in your automated sequence to help to build relationships and get the conversation started.
- **Reiterate key facts and points** - Just because you've mentioned a key point or benefit before, doesn't mean you can't again. In fact, reiterating your key unique selling points is a great way to ensure they get retained and not just instantly forgotten by the reader.
- **Keep your emails simple** - Don't try and get too clever or complicated in your messages, remember clarity beats cleverness.
- **Use dual-readership path** - As we've already mentioned the dual readership path means that people can scan read your message and still get the gist of what you're talking about, before potentially committing to read it in its entirety.
- **Get some inspiration** - For more inspiration, refer to the social media content guides on pages 99-108, as many of the same concepts can be used for any content that you create.

Setting Up The Automation

With all of your initial emails now written and in place, it's time to get them uploaded into your Automation sequence. Given the vast number of email software choices, it's not possible for me to dive into the instructional level, however, many systems do follow the same basic principles.

Automation / Auto Responders

The whole process of creating an automatic sequence of emails is frequently known as automation or an auto-responder. These are campaigns in which you can add multiple emails to be sent out in a particular sequence. The first step will be to create a campaign of this type.

Triggers

A trigger is an event which causes your automation to start. In the majority of instances, this will be that someone has successfully completed a particular web form and been added to your list.

Time Delays

Automation is usually controlled by time delays starting from the moment the trigger occurred. For example, the moment someone completes your web form, you would most likely wish to send the first email immediately. The email may contain a welcome email along with any digital deliverables like PDF guides, video links or coupon codes you may have promised. After this, you may wish to add a time delay for a given number of hours or days before sending your next message.

Email Sending Times

In many platforms you will be able to configure the time windows at which your emails are to be sent. People will subscribe at the strangest of times, like when they can't sleep and are still browsing the web at 3am. This would result in all of your emails being sent at 3am and would be a give away that your emails are automated. To get around this, you may only wish to send emails to your prospects during business hours to make it feel more in keeping with your usual business practice.

Internal Tasks And Emails

Emails to your prospects are the most common action. However, there is no reason why you couldn't add emails into your sequence which are sent to your staff to notify them to complete an internal task. If you've asked for a phone number, it might be an email sent to your sales rep to give this customer a follow-up call after they've just received an email about a special offer.

Advanced Features

Other more advanced features of automation will allow for actions commencing based on links being clicked, videos being watched and much more. These items can add a greater level of personalisation, but will only be available depending on the functionality of the software you are using.

How Many Emails Should Be Sent?

One of the most frequent questions we get asked with automation is "how many emails should I be writing and sending?". The answer I'm afraid is 'it depends'. The longer your sales cycle, the longer it would benefit your email sequence to be. Further to this, the frequency of when your emails are sent will denote how many emails you need to create.

The best tip is to start with a number, for example 10-15 emails and get them uploaded and live. You can easily add more emails at a later stage. If you're looking for a starting point, I would also start by testing either 1 or 2 emails each week and try adding more as you look for the sweet spot.

One thing to consider when planning for your frequency of emails is to bear in mind that prospects are 'hottest' when they first come into your sequence. So you may want to match this opportunity with a higher density of communication and slow it down as time passes.

Stopping The Automation

Depending on your requirements and the functionality of your software, it may be necessary to stop the sequence. For example, if your emails all relate to booking a free consultation. The moment they have booked it, you will want to either stop the sequence or move them into a different sequence. If this is an issue, then just make sure that your emails are kept generic and can be easily sent to both new prospects and existing customers alike.

Data Protection And GDPR

As of 25th May 2018, data protection laws in the EU changed, meaning you now have to comply with a number of conditions if you intend to collect contact information and use it for marketing.

Before I make these recommendations, I'd just like to state that I'm not a legal expert and not qualified to give legal advice in this area, so please ensure that you consult an expert on this subject before taking action.

Your whole local marketing system will be built around collecting contact details and marketing to these people. The law changes are not discouraging you from doing this, simply requesting that you follow some best practices.

- **Be clear about your intentions** - It's critical to be transparent with how you intend to use your prospect's data. Let them know that you intend to send them useful advice and sales related information that they can unsubscribe from at any point.
- **Ensure that anyone can opt-out** - Be sure to include an unsubscribe link at the bottom of every email that you send as part of your automation sequence. There is no benefit at all in sending marketing messages to someone who doesn't want to receive them.
- **Be responsible with your data** - As any business who has invested time and money into building their list will understand, it can be one of the most prof-

itable assets any business can own. Be sure to treat it this way. Make sure no third parties have access to your data.

CHAPTER 15

Re-Engagement
Step 9. Remarketing

So now we move into the last stage of the re-engagement phase, and another important step to maximising the number of leads you are able to capture.

Have you ever noticed banner adverts depicting products or businesses you have recently looked at, following you around the internet as you visit other websites?

This technique is known as Remarketing and is an extremely powerful way to get another chance with visitors who have recently been on your website but did not complete a goal.

As a small business, when you start investing in your online marketing, you'll quickly become frustrated by the number of visitors or clicks that you pay for who are not interested or don't take action when they first land on your website.

Even if you've ensured that the way you drive traffic is efficient, not having anything in place to give you a second 'bite at the cherry' can be the difference between winning and losing.

With more and more of your competitors realising the power of Remarketing, it will not only become more difficult to get attention, but it will be crucial that your message cuts through the noise and connects with the thoughts that are running around in your prospect's head.

The number of people that don't take action will always significantly outweigh the number who do, but if you have the right system in place, then your business will be able to increase profits from your initial spend, whilst maximising the number of leads available to you.

You can use Remarketing to squeeze each and every additional lead possible by continuing to show your message long after they've left your website.

Remarketing is a similar and complementary system to what we've already discussed with your Facebook ads, however, whilst Facebook is focused on Facebook and Instagram users, Remarketing takes care of the rest of the internet and is delivered using Google's Display Network (GDN).

What Is Remarketing?

Whenever someone visits your website, a small piece of data called a 'cookie' is stored on his or her computer or device. This data indicates to Google that your ads can potentially be shown to this user whilst they continue to browse other websites.

All of the people who have this cookie on their computer or device become your audience. The audience can be further broken down to only show your ads to people who have looked at a particular page on your website, or by restricting the websites on which your adverts can be displayed.

Your remarketing banner ads can be displayed automatically on millions of other people's websites.

An eye-catching banner advert should share your message and promote immediate action to get them back to your website.

Your banners may be shown on any website which is connected to the Google partner scheme depending on how relevant your ads are and how much you are prepared to pay for each click.

Advert placements are available in many different sizes from square through to tall or wide, which means a variation of each ad should be designed to fit each of the popular dimensions. It is possible to design 'responsive banners' which will automatically adjust to any placement size and even animated banners to further help your advert stand out.

Benefits Of Remarketing

- **Reduce marketing waste** - Remarketing is one of the best strategies to avoid losing people who have visited your website once but never completed a goal.
- **Increase conversion rate** - With more than one 'bite at the cherry' so to speak, it's inevitable that you will increase your overall conversion rate of customers who ultimately complete a goal.
- **Extremely cost effective** - Remarketing is designed to mop up prospects who slipped through the net. Although your adverts will be shown to many people, you're only paying for the small number of people who proceed to click on your ads.
- **Low-cost brand awareness** - The bonus benefit is that your ads are visually shown to larger numbers of people who may never click, giving you a fantastically low priced way of getting your brand in front of your prospects.
- **Eye-catching** - Banners can be designed to be visually striking and even include animation meaning you're able to truly stand out, even on an already crowded page.

Getting Started With Remarketing

Developing and maintaining a successful Remarketing campaign requires work in the following areas.

Banner Design

Remarketing adverts are visual designs and should be created with a number of factors in mind. Whilst being eye-catching and standing out from the page, they also need to 're-capture' the viewer's attention and remind them of the message/ offer which was previously described on the website they have recently visited.

As well as using familiar design styles, consistent with your original landing page, it should also include your 'call to action' as the aim is to drive people back to your website and finish completing the original goal.

Remarketing Banner Sizes

For your initial banner designs, I would recommend producing 20 banners. This is made up of 2 variations for the 10 most popular sizes. Here are the exact dimensions. *See page 157 for a diagram of all 10 sizes.*

Banner Types

There are three different types of banners which can be created and added to your remarketing campaign.

Image Banners

Image banners are the most common type of banner for your Remarketing campaign. They are the quickest to produce and are perfect for testing which images, styles and copy works the best.

10 most popular placement sizes for your initial remarketing banner adverts.

Animated Banners

Once your most effective messages have been established, you can then start to add subtle animation in order to ensure your banner advert has the maximum effectiveness and stands out on even the most crowded of pages.

Responsive Banners

All Remarketing banner placements are given exact dimensions for size. Responsive banners automatically adjust to fit the exact size. Responsive banners will ensure your best-performing banners can be shown in every available placement without creating lots of different versions. Responsive banners can be designed by downloading Google's Web Designer software available for free on both Mac and Windows.

Remarketing Banner Tips

To get the most from the Remarketing component of your local marketing system, here are some useful tips to keep you moving in the right direction.

- **Produce lots of banners and quickly** - Your ability to quickly produce banners and let the market decide, will end up being your secret weapon when it comes to improving your performance.
- **Test static banners first** - Before moving on to animated and responsive banners make sure you have thoroughly tested your message first. Be sure to keep your banner design and layout as close to identical as possible as you switch to animated and responsive banners.
- **One clear call to action** - Only use one clear call to action, too many different messages will confuse your readers. For best results keep your call to action exactly the same as what was on the landing page they have previously visited.
- **Clarity beats cleverness** - As I've mentioned on numerous occasions, it's our mantra to avoid being clever, as clarity will always win in marketing.
- **Include a call to action button** - Although with remarketing, the whole banner is usually clickable, it's worthwhile testing having an actual button drawn

to focus the viewer's attention and provide a clear place to click.

- **Don't be emotionally attached to your results** - With any piece of marketing which requires bespoke design, it can be easy to attach yourself to personal preference. This will likely cloud your ability to make decisions based on profitability alone.

- **Learn from your Google Ads testing plan** - Google Ads and Remarketing are very closely related, be sure to apply what you have learned from one component into the other.

- **Segment your audience** - If your website has a lot of traffic, you'll soon realise that remarketing to everybody can quickly become expensive and fruitless. You may just want to focus on people who have come via Google Ads or dedicated SEO landing pages.

Design Optimisation & Testing

Just like all other components of your local marketing system, an ongoing regimented testing plan for your banners is the only way to continually improve the performance.

Without further ado, let's move on to this all-important stage in the process, testing and optimisation.

CHAPTER 16

Optimise
Step 10. Testing & Optimisation

Well, now we've reached the final and arguably the most important section in the 10-step system.

If everything we've talked about this far is the bricks, then testing and optimisation is most certainly the mortar that holds everything together, keeping it strong and durable long into the future.

The best thing about digital marketing is the fact that you can see exactly what's going on at any given moment. A depth of intelligence that all other forms of marketing, such as newspaper adverts, flyers, and even television have never as yet been able to provide.

Testing your local marketing system is the difference between a nice gimmick and a proven lead generation machine. This is your chance to fine-tune the work that you've done and ensure that it helps to grow your business in the way that you so desire.

If you've ever played the guitar, then you'll know that even though so much blood, sweat and tears have gone into crafting the body, the neck and creating a beautiful finish, if the strings are not in tune, then the instrument is effectively useless. And it's exactly the same with your local marketing system.

Now there's good news. Just like tuning a guitar, it's actually a pretty straightforward process to tune your local marketing system too, especially when you have the right tools and know how to use them.

Analytics

The first tool is Google Analytics. Analytics is the tracking software that will keep an in-depth real-time record of every single visitor that lands on your website, blog or landing page. Armed with this data, you have the ability to dig deeper into finding out exactly what is happening with your marketing. Now don't be put off by the technical nature of this, as much of what we need to track is only scratching the surface of what Analytics is actually capable of.

The platform will detect the number of visitors, where they came from, what pages they viewed, how long they stayed on each page and even their age, gender and the location they are viewing from.

Before spending on any advertising, one of the biggest worries for any business owner is "will this actually work and help drive some business?". This is a question which many advertising channels might not be able to answer at all. Whereas, with online marketing and Google Analytics, we can safely say that we have all of the tools to make an extremely accurate assessment of both performance and return on investment.

Armed with real data, we no longer need to rely on 'experts' or even worse, mere guesswork, in order to get your website performing at the required rate. Furthermore, with the ability to closely track your marketing performance comes the ability to spot patterns and trends early and make informed decisions based on profit.

One final benefit is that Google Analytics is completely free to use and can be added to your website with very little effort. If you already have a website, chances are it's probably already tracking with Google Analytics as it is usually added by your web designer.

Installing Google Analytics

Getting Analytics tracking on your website is simple and only requires a small snippet of code to be added to each page. Ask your website designer to do this for you, or if you use Wordpress, you'll find several plugins which can do this on your behalf.

It's also advisable to ensure your account is connected to both Google Ads and Google Search Console. This will mean that your data can be shared between these platforms to give you maximum insight.

Setting Up Trackings Goals

Once your tracking code is live and tracking visitors, it's now important to add some context to your data. For this, you'll need to outline what your key marketing objectives are. For most businesses looking for more local customers, it would usually be considered that a successful action would be a visitor filling out an online form to provide their contact details. Further to this, it may also be worth tracking the number of people that click to make a phone call, or request a download by clicking a button.

Once you've outlined each of your goals, you can set them up in Analytics. There are two main ways to achieve this:

1. **Page URL visit** - This goal type will be triggered when a user reaches a particular page. The target URL should match that of the 'thank you' page to which your users are directed after the successful completion of a goal.
2. **Event Tracking** - An event occurs when a particular action takes place. Events can be triggered at any point including when a button has been clicked by the user. These events can then be tracked as a goal.

Make sure that each of your goals is not only set up but also tested to ensure that data is actually tracking before getting started. It can take a few hours for data to feed back into the system.

Key Metrics

Understanding exactly what every piece of data means isn't critical to your success. However, there are a number of extremely important figures you have to watch with an eagle eye, as they will give you an exact reading of how well your marketing and business is performing.

It's only possible to track your performance online to the point of submitting a lead. In order to get the full picture, it's strongly recommended to track up to the point of sale and beyond. This can either be done automatically using a CRM tool or manually in a spreadsheet. I've outlined some key metrics which you will need to get your head around and closely follow at all times:

- **Cost per lead (also by traffic source)** - Each and every component of your marketing system will cost you in either money or time, so being able to identify which is providing the best return is critical for monitoring your success. Cost per lead is how much you have to spend on your marketing to get each lead. This should take into consideration any advertising spend and agency fees.
- **Cost per customer (also by traffic source)** - Not all of the leads generated by your local marketing system will turn into paying customers. Working out how many of your leads turned into buyers will allow you to calculate your cost per customer. It's also worth calculating this by traffic source for a clear picture of individual performance.
- **Average order value (AOV)** - By tracking each sale, you should be able to calculate the average amount of money that someone spends when they place an order with you. This figure will help you to estimate how much you can spend to get each order.
- **Customer Lifetime Value (CLTV)** - There is a lot of hidden value to your marketing if your customers go on to place repeat purchases from your business. The average customer lifetime value totals the average of what each customer spends with you throughout their lifetime and can help to predict what is likely to happen in the future. Having this information will add context to what you can afford to spend to buy a new customer.

AB Testing

We speak with so many businesses who come to us after having dabbled in online marketing but never got the results they desired. They feel that everything is a risk and they don't know if it's going to work. These fears are true to some extent, but mostly there is a way to guarantee that your local marketing system will work.

There is a way to ensure that each time you conduct some work, you will either make your campaign slightly better or succeed in identifying a way which doesn't work that you can now confidently avoid. This process is called 'testing' and is the magic fairy dust needed to make your local marketing system take to the skies.

When I say magic fairy dust, I'm actually referring to what your competitors will think you have once you get this stuff working, but as with all success in online marketing, it's completely down to systemically establishing what works and doing more of it.

So we've already talked about testing on numerous occasions in the book in many of the sections so far. Allow this perpetual referencing to underpin exactly how valuable it is when it comes to unlocking the true power in your marketing.

What Is AB Testing?

Just to recap, split testing or AB testing is the process of taking two similar variations of a web page or advert and tracking to see which one converts more of your visitors based on your defined goals.

With every single pound you invest into marketing your business you have two distinct opportunities. The first and most obvious opportunity is to generate more leads, sales and ultimately profit. However, it's the second opportunity that most businesses are simply oblivious to. It's the ability to continually improve the performance of your campaign using the most valuable data possible; real-life data from people looking to give you money.

The end result means we can make decisions in a scientific way, based only on actual evidence and not on emotion, preference or our own egotistical bias.

The vast majority of business owners feel they are more than capable of understanding what their customers want, like or need. Whilst you are positioned based on your experience to have a very good idea, none of us are smart enough to know this for sure.

And the point is, there is no reason to try to guess when you can get real-life evidence from the very people that matter most, your customers.

Getting Started With AB Testing

Throughout the next few pages of this chapter, you're going to learn the tools and techniques to be able to start running your very own AB testing experiments with ease. Creating your first experiment begins with choosing your software.

As with most areas we've covered so far, the aim is to help you get started quickly. Although there are a number of software options, I'm going to focus on Google Optimize. Optimize is the latest revision of Google's offering when it comes to split testing. A few years back, Google used to have a system known as Website Optimizer which was its free software for running split tests. It later discontinued this and opted to combine the functionality with Google Experiments which became an add-on for Google Analytics.

As of 2017, it has once again released a standalone package, but this time it's much better positioned to compete with other offerings on the market.

I'd recommend starting with Optimize as it's not only free, it's also easy to integrate with other components of your local marketing system.

The software works by allowing you to load a page on your website, and subsequently make a variation of this without touching any of your website code. Once you are happy with this, you can set the experiment live. This means that you can have tests running in a matter of minutes, without any expensive development and in minimum time.

Setting Up Google Optimize

All you need to do to get started is to get the code added to your website. Just like with your Google Analytics code or Facebook Pixel, this is probably best to be added by your website designer.

Once your code is added to your website and tracking is actively working, the next step is to connect your Google Analytics and Google Ads accounts. This will help to ensure that you have the most meaningful data for your experiment and also be able to analyse your results in more depth as part of Google Analytics.

Creating Your First Experiment

Now you're ready to start running your first test. Before we dive in, it's important to ensure that you are best prepared.

Decide Which Component To Test

Before you even think about running an experiment, you need to identify which component of your local marketing you will need to test. This could be a Google Ads, SEO or Facebook ads landing page. You will be able to identify the areas of your system which look like they are underperforming by carefully monitoring your key metrics. If you don't have enough data, I would recommend starting with your highest traffic pages. These pages will have the most opportunity for getting data quickly, and will also be your most valuable pages. These findings will provide the fastest results and can always be rolled out across other pages of the website if the results are positive.

Here are a few testing ideas to get you started:

- **Learn from previous test data** - The first and best places to look are the tests that you might have already run as part of your Google Ads testing data or on other pages. Testing will naturally lead on to future testing ideas.

- **Insights from customers** - Run surveys or make phone calls to identify the needs or requests of your customers. They may provide extremely valuable insight into why they bought and how they envision your customer experience can be improved.

- **Heatmap tracking** - Heatmap recordings will allow you to playback actual videos of website visitors as they browsed your site, and identify areas which they might have missed, skipped, ignored or been confused by. This is a great way to identify potential problems and areas to test next. Heat map tracking can be easily added to your website using HotJar.

- **Learn from other industries** - Breakthroughs often happen from outside your own industry. This means things that are working for businesses in different industries to your own may also work in your business. Spend some time looking to identify how successful websites attract leads outside of your sector. This could include the kind of promotions they are running or the 'customer journey' steps they encourage their visitors to take.

- **Get a little helping hand** - Just to get you off to the very best possible start, we've included 100 experience-based ideas to provide some inspiration for tests, which are listed later in this chapter.

Produce A Hypothesis

If you think back to when you used to do science experiments in your chemistry lessons, you'd first create a hypothesis and then conduct the experiment to prove your hypothesis to be true or false. The exact same is true for running your AB testing experiments.

So before we get started let's recap on what a hypothesis is, I'm happy to excuse you if your GCSE science is a little rusty.

A hypothesis is a prediction that is made prior to commencing with an experiment. It should clearly state exactly what is being tested, why you think it will make a change and what you think the outcome will be. Then by running the experiment, you will be able to either prove or disprove your hypothesis.

The reason for this doing this first is that we need to ensure that every test is carried out on the back of a solid principle rather than random hope.

How Long Should I Run Tests For?

Once your test is up and running the next consideration is how long the test should be running for. Without going into the depths of statistical analysis, there a few key concepts which you need to be aware of. The idea of testing is to *statistically identify the likelihood of a particular outcome*. The longer the test runs for and the more test subjects we put through it, the more accurate the final prediction.

Given this, when deciding how long you should run your tests, it should really depend on how much traffic your landing page currently receives. This aside, you should also consider seasonality of your data, meaning that you may have different traffic levels and conversion rates for each day of the week, so it's critical that all tests run for at least a week.

If your traffic levels are low, you might want to try running this for a full month. In an ideal world, you should be running for a sample size of 1000 people.

It's also worth noting that testing for too long can also be damaging as it can mean lost money on bad performing tests and also a lost opportunity to run further tests.

How To Choose A Winner

With your experiment now almost complete, it's time to decide if your test found a winner or not. For your landing page experiments, the calculation for working out winners is taken care of by Google Optimize and provided in your results data.

As a general rule of thumb, we would recommend that a winner should be chosen if it receives 95% certainty or above.

It's important to allow your test to run until the end even if you have a hunch that your hypothesis will prove true. It's natural to get emotionally attached to your bias. Google takes into consideration not only statistical significance but also typical user behaviour differences on recently updated websites.

Once you have a winner, you'll then be able to roll these results out to the live site and potentially across the remainder of any landing pages where these results could also be applicable.

Recording Your Results

As with any project you are working on, getting the best results will directly relate to how well organised your approach is. Simply randomly running tests may result in some improvement, however, it's most likely to result in you gradually losing interest, especially if you've had a few back-to-back fails.

The best approach is to manage your testing by keeping a simple spreadsheet with the following fields:

- Test Number (ID)
- Test Name
- Test Hypothesis / Description
- Date Started
- Date Ended
- Result
- Certainty (% certainty of the test beating the original (also called 'control'))

Set yourself either a regular testing day or perhaps commit to running a total number of split tests over a given period of time. This will give you a clear goal, whilst helping to keep a structured and organised approach.

You can always think of a few tests in advance to help you plan ahead with your strategy. A structured approach to testing like this could make a huge difference to your overall bottom line.

Further to this, you'll have a record of every test completed so that you can use and learn from this data in other components of your local marketing system.

Don't Give Up

Like anything in life, your ability to stick to the program will be the most important aspect of your final success. Statistically speaking, most of your tests will fail, but remember, it's important to view each test as a mini-victory because you are successfully identifying ideas which work as well as ones which don't.

Also, bear in mind that your competitors are most likely not even aware of testing, let alone running a comprehensive testing program.

100 Things To Split Test

Here are a 100 things that you can use to get started with your testing programme.

Images

1. People vs products
2. Stock images vs real photos
3. Photos of real staff *(try adding photos of your actual team to your pages)*
4. Gender images *(images of men vs women)*
5. Demographics images *(images based on the age, race, income, interests of your customer profile)*
6. Static image vs animated GIF
7. Test background images

Typeface

8. Serif vs sans-serif *(test different font styles)*
9. Font sizes
10. Font colours
11. Different fonts *(test individual fonts)*

Copywriting

12. The tone of your writing style
13. Short headlines vs longer headlines
14. Paragraph text vs bullet point list
15. Positive vs negative messaging (*e.g. make more money v stop wasting your money*)
16. Long form copy vs short form copy
17. Written copy vs video
18. Power words (Google "power words")
19. Use of the word FREE
20. Personal stories or case studies
21. Scarcity (*e.g. booking up fast, not many left, don't miss out*)
22. Urgency (*e.g. act now, deadlines, countdown timers etc.*)
23. The priority of benefits from your message
24. Use of key problems identified in your message
25. USP variations
26. The order of words in your headlines
27. Use numbers (*e.g. 4 instead of four*)
28. Use accurate numbers rather than generalised (*e.g. 3863 subscribers, not almost 4000 subscribers*)
29. Use capitalisation
30. Speed of delivery (*e.g. completed in 24 hours*)
31. Speed/ease of completion (*e.g. complete this form in 20 seconds*)
32. Adding a P.S to your sales copy to reiterate key points
33. Adding polarisation (*Who this is not for*)

Pricing And Offers

34. Pricing
35. Pricing packages/tiers
36. Pricing vs no pricing
37. Free trial/free consultation/free sample

38. One product vs multiple product options

Lead Magnet

39. Names for your lead magnet
40. Mockup images of your lead magnet
41. Changing the contents of your offer

Call To Action Button

42. Changing the colour
43. Changing the style
44. Changing the shape of the button
45. Changing the text on the button
46. Changing the positioning
47. Repeating the call to action throughout your page
48. Animating the call to action
49. Adding arrows and navigational cues pointing at your call to action
50. Add white space around the call to action
51. Use of possessive pronouns in button text *(e.g. Get My Free Guide vs Get Your Free Guide)*
52. Direct instruction in button text "click here to…"
53. Exit intent popup *(a popup form which appears when people are about to leave your website)*

Web Forms

54. Offer lead magnet vs quick contact form
55. Visible contact form vs popup form when a button is clicked
56. Number of form fields
57. Size/style of your fields
58. Forms with or without photos
59. Required fields vs non-required fields

Videos

60. Changing the content/messaging
61. Adding video captions
62. Changing video thumbnails
63. Autoplay (without sound) vs click to play

Page Layouts

64. Removing your navigation/header element
65. Removing distractions from your page
66. Single column layout vs main column with sidebar
67. The ordering of your navigation links
68. Names of your navigation links
69. Number of steps in your lead generation sales funnel
70. Colours of your page elements
71. Social sharing buttons style
72. Social sharing buttons positioning
73. Test text vs icons for key page elements

Technical

74. Page loading time improvements
75. Loading iFrame videos on click rather than page load
76. Location-targeted pages (e.g. area written in landing page copy)
77. Fixed call to action scrolling with the page
78. SSL certificate types
79. Use of live chat

Social proof

80. Use of different customer reviews
81. Written reviews vs video reviews
82. Ratings from different providers, e.g. Google, TripAdvisor, TrustPilot etc

83. Adding a guarantee
84. Length of guarantee *(e.g. 30 days vs 90 days)*
85. Labels *(e.g. bestseller, most popular)*
86. Awards and accreditation logos
87. Existing customers logos
88. Security and safety symbols

Google Ads

89. Landing page URL paths
90. Headline copy
91. Call to actions
92. Use of Ad extensions

Email

93. Subject lines
94. Subject line length
95. Questions in your subject line *(e.g. Can I Ask A Favour?)*
96. The frequency of sending emails *(e.g. daily, weekly, monthly)*
97. Sender name, branded or personal contact
98. Time of day sending *(e.g. AM vs PM)*
99. Dynamic content in emails *(e.g. use of name and company name in the email body text)*
100. Video in email

Planned Account Management

OK, time for a quick reality check. Simply knowing this stuff isn't going to be enough, even setting it up isn't enough, the only thing that will work is to tend to this on a regular basis, just like a farmer tends to his crops, week after week, year after year.

This is where you will start to see the benefit of being able to manage your team and ensure that work is consistently produced in accordance with your plan.

Set certain days aside each month to work on tweaking each component of your local marketing system so that you can keep your results and performance consistent.

The time you invest here will be what generates profit for your business further down the line.

Create A Work Schedule

The best place to start will be to create a work schedule. Take a blank piece of paper in landscape orientation and draw a table broken into four columns. Each of the four columns represents a week of the month, four weeks in total. Now plot each of the components of your system into each allotted week.

By planning out pre-arranged slots where you can work on the optimisation of each component, you can then commit to a routine and to building a positive habit. If you are delegating this work to your team, ensure they are clear about their responsibilities and keep you regularly updated with progress reports along the way.

CHAPTER 17

Getting Started

"The best time to plant a tree is twenty years ago. The second best time is now."

- Chinese Proverb

Well, congratulations for making it this far. By reaching this stage, you are already leaps and bounds ahead of most other businesses and more importantly your competitors.

Now you have everything you need to be able to generate a consistent flow of leads into your business on a regular basis, you can start to make great strides towards achieving your long-term business goals.

Lots of business owners buy books, but leave them unread and gathering dust. So by reaching the end, I already know you are serious about making a change in your business and life. Whilst many successful entrepreneurs can list the best books they've read, the elite few will also be able to tell you what they implemented as a result of reading each book.

The Next 12 Months Are Critical

Before you return this book to your bookshelf or lend it to a friend, get a pen and paper and flick back through each section of the book to make a note of everything that you intend to implement in your business over the next 12 months.

Many people frequently overestimate what they can get done in a day, but massively underestimate, what they can achieve in a year.

Your next move needs to be a smart one. Just before we finish, I want to recap on a few very important truths we've learned along the way:

- This system has been developed over the last decade and more importantly based on one very simple principle - *only do what works!*
- Yes, it's going to be harder than you might imagine to get it working.
- Yes, you are going to make mistakes along the way, but make them quickly and continue moving forward.
- It doesn't have to be perfect it just has to be started.

If you want any further help with anything that's mentioned in this book, or if you want to share your results, then we would absolutely love to hear from you.

You can reach us at support@gowebsites.co.uk or by phone on 0333 777 5050.

Good luck.

Printed in Great Britain
by Amazon